# ERICH FRAUWALLNER'S
# POSTHUMOUS ESSAYS

Translated from the German by
JAYANDRA SONI

ADITYA PRAKASHAN
New Delhi

ISBN 81-85689-99-7



First published in 1994

Published by Pradeep Kumar Goel for Aditya Prakashan
F-14/65, Model Town II, Delhi – 110 009
and printed at Crescent Printing Works Pvt. Ltd.,
P-14, Connaught Circus, New Delhi – 110 001

## Table of Contents

## Translator's Note

Erich Frauwallner has the enviable reputation of being extremely clear in his writing. Further, in his translations of Sanskrit texts he strives earnestly to be true to the original. I have attempted the same attitude in my translation of his German. I have also retained his method of transliteration; hence the use of Nyāyaḥ, Vaiśeṣikam, etc., whenever he uses them.

Frauwallner does not use italics when referring to books, as I have done here. Apart from this, the form is exactly the same as in the original German publicaton. In some places, especially in the preliminary remarks and particularly for titles of articles, I have repeated the German, in which cases the English has been given in simple brackets. Further, Frauwallner often refers to his two volumes on the history of Indian philosophy as Vol. I or Vol. II. These have already been translated into English and I have supplied the corresponding page numbers – see p. 131 for the bibliographical details.

Every translation has to cope with the problem of rendering the nuances of a language as truly as is at all possible. In this regard my wife Dr. Luitgard Soni has struggled with me to find the approporiate English equivalents and I am indebted to this laborious assistance. I have also received valuable recommendations and suggestions from my friends Mr. Jürgen Hanneder M.A., Mr. Johannes Schneider M.A. and Mr. Roland Steiner M.A., all of whom are Ph.D. candidates in the field of Indology at the University of Marburg, Germany.

I especially thank Prof. Dr. Ernst Steinkellner for the permission to translate the original German book which he edited under the title: *Erich Frauwallner Nachgelassene Werke I: Aufsätze, Beiträge, Skizzen* which was published in Vienna in 1984. I also thank him for the final approval of the translation.

Jayandra Soni
University of Marburg
Department of Indology
D-35032 Marburg, Germany

December 1993

## Foreword

Erich Frauwallner, Emeritus-Professor of "Indische Philologie und Altertumskunde" (Indian Philology and Antiquity), member of the "Österreichische Akademie der Wissenschaften" (Austrian Academy of the Sciences), correspondent member of the "Akademie der Wissenschaften zu Göttingen" (Academy of the Sciences in Göttingen) and honorary member of the "Deutsche Morgenländische Gesellschaft" (German Oriental Scociety) died in Vienna on July 5, 1974.

Professor Frauwallner's academic bequest consists of two parts: of a library and of writings. The library could be bought for the University of Vienna through an endowment granted by the Austrian Ministry for "Wissenschaft und Forschung" (Science and Research) and was incorporated in the collections of the "Institut für Indologie" and the "Institut für Tibetologie und Buddhismuskunde". In accordance with Frauwallner's wishes the writings were first entrusted to the editor by his daughters, Ortrun Zangenberg and Irmgard Igel, and then finally on November 1, 1975, they were donated to the Institut für Tibetologie und Buddhismuskunde. In the years 1976-1977 these posthumous writings were arranged and catalogued as a collection with the help of the Fund for the Promotion of Scientific Research in Austria.

Professor Frauwallner's posthumous writings consist essentially of four parts: 1. "Collections of Material", which are mainly photocopies and hand-written copies of texts, especially of the epistemological-logical school of Buddhism; 2. "Working texts", which consist of analyses of literature, systematic notes and reading notes; 3. "Translations" in connection with the "History of Indian Philosophy" and 4. Complete and incomplete "presentations".

As a first step, only those texts of the bequest are being considered for publication which Frauwallner himself had already decided to have published. Out of the remaining material only useful supplements to these texts are to be published.

This first volume of the posthumous works contains all the complete and incomplete presentations of various working periods which remained pending for different reasons. The preliminary remarks to each of the texts furnish some detailed information. The second volume that is planned is "Texte indischer Philosophie in Übersetzung" (Texts of Indian Philosophy in Translation), to be edited by Gerhard Oberhammer. The third volume will contain selected drafts and incomplete notes to the first part of the planned volume three of the "History of Indian Philosophy", which was to deal with the origin of the Hīnayāna systems.

Apart from simple corrections to the manuscripts, no changes in the content nor in the style have been made in this present volume of published texts. Incomplete references have been supplemented, references to literature have been partly modified because Frauwallner very often used editions of texts that are accessible nowadays only with great diffculty. All supplementations are in square brackets. Bracketed references such as [R/II/1], refer to the collection of the bequest: File R, Book II, Page 1 ("Mappe R, Heft II, Seite 1").

Special thanks of the editor are due to Mrs. Ortrun Zangenberg and Mrs. Irmgard Igel who, through their generous gift, have made possible the care of his revered teacher's bequest.

Ernst Steinkellner

# I.

## On the Historical Value of the Ancient Ceylonese Chronicles

## [R/I/1 - R/I/28]

### Preliminary Remarks

According to the dating of the manuscript, the hand-written fair copy of the introduction and of the first chapter were begun on May 15, 1952 [R/I/1] and finished on May 26, 1952 [R/I/10]. The rest is undated because the fair copy was unfinished. However, the writing and the paper are of the same kind as in the first part. So, this article belongs to the same time as "Die buddhistischen Konzile" (ZDMG 102, 1952, 240-261 "The Buddhists Councils") and the printed lecture "Die ceylonesischen Chroniken und die erste buddhistische Mission nach Hinterindien" ("The Ceylonese Chronicles and the first Buddhist Mission to Hinter-India") at the "IVe Congrès International des Sciences Anthropologiques et Ethnologiques, Vienne 1952" (Actes, Tome II, 1955, 192-197). While the article abòut the Councils had already been given for print during the time of the fair copy (reference to ZDMG on R/I/27, note 20), the lecture for the congress, which took place September 1-8, 1952, was written only after the essay published here.

The summarized analysis and assessment of the historical tradition of Ceylon contained in the first part of the above lecture, is based on the present essay in which the analysis is presented in detail.

The essay originally bore the title "Über die Glaubwürdigkeit der ceylonesischen Chroniken" ("On the Credibility of the Ceylonese Chronicles"), which was however corrected in pencil.

On the basis of the available notes it is possible to make supplementations beyond the end of the fair copy. For the whole of the last section "Die Kirchengeschichte des Mutterlandes" ("The Church History of the Motherland") there is a draft on pages R/II/1 and R/II/2 under the title "Mutterländische Kirchengeschichte" ("Motherland Church History"). The beginning of this draft, upto the note "Moggaliputta Schulhaupt" ("Moggaliputta, the Head of the School") is elaborated in the fair copy. In this draft the text given in Appendix A [R/II/1] then follows.

The last line of the draft "leads to general questions and insights" shows that Frauwallner here became aware of the comprehensive problem of the tradition of the motherland, and that he began with the work which led to his *The Earliest Vinaya and the Beginnings of Buddhist Literature* (Rome, 1956), which was actually completed by the end of 1953. That he had the intention, after completing this additional work, to finish the article about the chronicles, is evident from a comment at the end of the work on the Vinaya (loc.cit., p. 171). The reason why he however did not again take up the work on the chronicles - according to a passing remark during a walk in 1968 or 1969 - was the awareness that with his manner of working every destraction from his actual theme - at that time the comprehensive presentation of the history of Indian philosophy - would demand too much time. And, that in order to avoid this danger, it seemed worthwhile to him, to leave incomplete the already developed article on the chronicals.

Another page with a draft [R/II/11] indicates how the article was to progress further. After the analysis of the sources the "Beurteilung der Quellen" ("Assessment of the Sources") was to follow and, moreover, a section "Fragen der Nirvāṇa Ära" ("Questions of the Nirvāṇa Era") and a "Zusammenfassung" ("Summary"). Apart from this, the reference to "Appendix I" [p. 15] shows that one or several appendices were planned, of which the first was to have dealt with the Buddhaghosa legend. However, no such appendices are available.

In addition to Appendix A, I am including Appendix B, "Zusammensetzung des alten Mahāvaṃsa" ("The Composition of the Ancient Mahāvaṃsa") from Frauwallner's supplementary material [R/II/11].

In his fair copy Frauwallner referred to the literature according to the numbers of a bibliography which is unfortunately not available. Since this bibliography apparently contained more titles than are mentioned in the available fragment, I have accordingly replaced this reference system.

*

With the great significance attached to the Ceylonese chronicles, not only for the history of Ceylon but, above all, also for the history of Buddhism, it is no wonder that the question of its credibility has been often and vehemently expressed. The opinions range from far-reaching trust to outright scepsis. Nevertheless, it is a well-known rule that the credibility of extensive and very complex historical works should not be judged without distinction. It is more important that the individual parts be distinguished, checked in terms of the origin and accordingly evaluated. In dealing with the Ceylonese chronicles this, however, has been done so far only in a modest way. At present one cannot speak of a conscious and consistent implementation of this task. It is therefore attempted in the following to take the research in this area at least a few steps further. And I am beginning with the work done by W. Geiger, which continues to be basic, and especially with his book *Dīpavaṃsa und Mahāvaṃsa und die geschichtliche Überlieferung in Ceylon*,

Leipzig, 1905 ("The Dīpavaṃsa and the Mahāvaṃsa and the Historical Tradition in Ceylon").[1]

The *Dīpavaṃsa,* the historical introduction to Buddhaghosa's *Samantapāsādikā* and the *Mahāvaṃsa* constitute the subject of my investigation. The oldest of these works, the *Dīpavaṃsa*, leads into the history of Ceylon until the rule of Mahāsena (c.334-362 AD) and was perhaps written not too long afterwards. Buddhaghosa's *Samantapāsādikā*, which was translated into Chinese already in 489 AD, quotes the *Dīpavaṃsa*, and so its date is fixed within narrow limits. This also agrees with the tradition according to which Buddhaghosa's activities falls within the reign of Mahānāma who had sent a legation to China in 428 AD. The *Mahāvaṃsa,* finally, is a revision of the material of the *Dīpavaṃsa* which was composed by a certain Monk Mahānāma under the orders of King Dhātusena (516-526 AD).

We know that the source of all these three works is the ancient Singhalese *Aṭṭhakathā*. But this itself needs to be clarified. The term Aṭṭhakathā signifies an entire group of literature, namely, the ancient commentaries to the sacred writings of the Buddhist canon, written in the Singhalese language. Geiger had also rightly recognized this and had even sometimes clearly expressed it.[2] However, in his efforts to determine the sources of the *Mahāvaṃsa* he often tends to see the Aṭṭhakathā as a single work to which he relates the various accounts[3] and, thus, this Aṭṭhakathā has become a multifaceted, hardly imaginable monster in his hands. Our first task, therefore, is to determine which Aṭṭhakathā lies at the basis of each of the three mentioned works, and how it was composed.

---

[1] Henceforth: *Dīpavaṃsa und Mahāvaṃsa.* The English translation is by E.M. Coomaraswamy, Colombo, 1908. Later, G.P. Malalasekera included significant additions and amendments, especially in the introduction to his edition of the *Vaṃsatthappakāsinī,* which however does not essentially surpass the work done by Geiger.

[2] Eg., in *The Mahāvaṃsa or The Great Chronicle of Ceylon,* tr. into English, London 1912, X: "The Aṭṭhakathā, i.e., the old commentary-literature on the canonical writings of the Buddhists which Buddhaghosa took as a basis for his illuminating works". [I thank Professor Bechert of Göttingen for identifying this quotation].

[3] Especially striking is *Dīpavaṃsa und Mahāvaṃsa* 49; that is why he also finds two pages later the quotation from the *Majjhimasaṅgītiyā Cūḷasīhanādasuttavaṇṇanā Sīhalaṭṭhakathā* so difficult to understand.

The most valuable aid for this purpose is the already mentioned commentary to the *Mahāvaṃsa*, the *Vaṃsatthappakāsinī*. This is the work of an unknown author and was most probably written not too long after the *Mahāvaṃsa* itself, presumably around 700 AD.[4] Its value lies, above all, in the fact that the author still had access to the entire ancient commentary-literature in Singhalese and that he could furnish a wealth of quotations from it, which allowed him to draw the various conclusions regarding the form and content of those works. These quotations were carefully collected and dealt with, first by Geiger (loc.cit., pp. 47-57) and then, following his procedure, by Malalasekera (loc.cit., pp. LVI-LXXII). Most of them are, of course, from the basic text *Mahāvaṃsa*, although several other source works are mentioned as well. And since precisely here the question of the source of the *Mahāvaṃsa* is frought with all possible kinds of problems, we shall first turn to one of these other source works.

## 1. The Source of the Introduction to Buddhaghosa's *Samantapāsādikā*

The author of the *Vaṃsatthappakāsinī* pays special attention to the relation of the *Mahāvaṃsa* to its sources and he especially emphasizes it when Mahānāma deviates from his usual main source, the *Mahāvaṃsaṭṭhakathā*. In the process he mentions a *Vinayaṭṭhakathā* four times, and it is noteworthy that the details he gives about this *Vinayaṭṭhakathā* correspond almost throughout with the account in the introduction to the *Samantapāsādikā*.[5]

---

[4] As for the date of the *Vaṃsatthappakāsinī* I agree largely with the views of Malalasekera (G.P. Malalasekera, ed., *Vaṃsathappakāsinī Commentary on the Mahāvaṃsa*, 2 vols., London 1935, Vol. I, Introduction, CIV-CXI). Geiger's later dating, between 1000 and 1250 (loc.cit., 37), is exclusively based on the completely unfounded assumption that the *Mahābodhivaṃsakathā*, quoted on pp. 412, 9ff., is identical with the extant Pāli *Mahābodhivaṃsa*. On the other hand, as Malalasekera appropriately remarks, it is hardly to be supposed that the ancient Singhalese commentaries were extant so late and that they were available to readers. Moreover, only because of the immediate impact of the schism in the church under King Dāṭhopatissa II (642-651 AD) mentioned in *Vaṃsatthappakāsinī* 176, one would give so great an importance to this event that one would place it together with the formation of the large sects Dhammarūcika and Sāgalika.

[5] Geiger (loc.cit., p. 53) has overlooked this. Malalasekera (loc.cit., pp. LXVII f.) indeed noticed it but omitted to further evaluate the observation.

*Mahāvaṃsa* V, v. 81 relates that King Asoka used to spend 500 thousand coins daily, 100 thousand each for the Buddha, for the doctrine, for the order, for Thera Nigrodha and for the sick. *Vaṃsatthappakāsinī* (207, 16f.) notes that this report is taken from the *Vinayaṭṭhakathā* and not from the *Mahāvaṃsaṭṭhakathā*. The same report is also in the *Samantapāsādikā* (52, 20-27), whereas the *Dīpavaṃsa*, which usually reiterates the *Mahāvaṃsa* tradition most accurately, speaks of 400 thousand coins, 100 thousand each for the Cetiya worship, for preaching by the teachers, for the sick and for the order (VII, v. 46f.; c/f. also VII, v. 11f.; VI, v. 56).

*Mahāvaṃsa* XII, v. 52 reports that at the conversion of Suvaṇṇabhūmi by Theras Sonaka and Uttara, three and a half thousand young men and one and a half thousand girls renounced the world. *Vaṃsatthappakāsinī* (319, 13-15) notes that this number of one and a half thousand girls is mentioned only in the *Vinayaṭṭhakathā*, whereas the *Mahāvaṃsaṭṭhakathā* speaks only of twelve and a half thousand people in general. Here too, the *Samantapāsādikā* (69, 8-11) gives the same figure as the *Vinayaṭṭhakathā*.[6]

In *Mahāvaṃsa* XIV, v. 3 it is related that the deity which wanted to lure King Devānampiyatissa to go hunting near Mahinda, took on the form of a *gokaṇṇa*. The *Vaṃsatthappakāsinī* (329, 21f.) says that according to the *Vinayaṭṭhakathā* the form was that of a *rohitamiga*. Even *Samantapāsādikā* (73, 17) speaks of a *rohitamiga*, whereas the the *Dīpavaṃsa* (XII, v.45) speaks of a *gokaṇṇa*.

*Mahāvaṃsa* XV, v. 188-194, finally reports how King Devānampiyatissa drew the border of Tissārāma and how accordingly Mahinda fixed the border (*nimitta*). On this the *Vaṃsatthappakāsinī* (362, 3-5) remarks that exact details about each border are not given here because they are found in both the *Mahāvaṃsaṭṭhakathā* and the *Vinayaṭṭhakathā*. A corresponding description is lacking in the *Samantapāsādikā*, and it is precisely at this point that Buddhaghosa seems to have shortened his presentation.[7] In the *Dīpavaṃsa* (XIV, vv. 20-40) the drawing of the border is also described, even though not in any particular detail.

Thus, it is clear that in three cases the description of the *Samantapāsādikā* agrees with the *Vinayaṭṭhakathā* quoted in the *Vaṃsatthap-*

---

[6] The short report in the *Dīpavaṃsa* does not mention any figure at all.

[7] See below p. 27f.

*pakāsinī*. There is no deviation in the fourth case either. Only in the *Samantapāsādikā* the report in question is not recorded. However, we know that the *Samantapāsādikā* is a revision of a Aṭṭhakathā written in the Singhalese language and since this presentation was obviously an Aṭṭhakathā to the Vinaya, the conclusion is justified that it is the same *Vinayaṭṭhakathā* which is quoted in the *Vaṃsatthappakāsinī*.[8] And since, further, as Buddhaghosa himself says (2, 15ff.), his work is based on the *Aṭṭhakathā* of Mahāvihāra and that he only occasionally draws from other sources, and since in his work Mahānāma too relies largely on the writings of Mahāvihāra, we may see in it the *Vinayaṭṭhakathā* of Mahāvihāra.

In this way, the source of the introduction to the *Samantapāsādikā* is decided. It is, further, incorrect when Geiger thinks (*Dīpavaṃsa und Mahāvaṃsa*, p. 78) that the *Samantapāsādikā* and *Mahāvaṃsa* draw from the same source, because the *Mahāvaṃsaṭṭhakathā* and the *Vinayaṭṭhakathā* are contrasted as different works in the *Vaṃsatthappakāsinī*, and the source of the *Samantapāsādikā* is not the *Mahāvaṃsaṭṭhakathā* but the *Vinayṭṭhakathā* of Mahāvihāra.

Now, for the second question, namely, what did this source look like in detail. Does Buddhaghosa represent it faithfully in his *Samantapāsādikā*, or does he deviate from it more or less drastically? In order to answer this question we need to investigate the description of the *Samantapāsādikā* more closely. It contains the history of the tradition of the doctrine from the death of the Buddha until the founding of the local Ceylonese tradition and, in the main, incorporates the following events: the councils at Rājagaha, Vesālī and Pāṭaliputta, the despatching of missions, the conversion of Ceylon, the founding of the first monastery, the building of the first *thūpa* and the planting of the Bodhi tree. We shall first consider the history of the first two councils because there is a separate source for them which Buddhaghosa himself repeatedly quotes, namely, the council reports in the *Cullavagga*.

It is generally assumed that Buddhaghosa drew from the *Cullavagga* for this part of his description, and even Geiger holds this view (loc.cit., pp. 78f.). According to him "Buddhaghosa's report of the first council is based on Cullavagga XI, 1-8. He takes over whole sections from his source literally and elaborates them more in detail, presumably on the basis of the Singhalese Aṭṭhakathā". This is incorrect and is

---

[8] C/f. also Malalasekera, loc.cit. LVII f.

based on an inaccurate observation. Rather, Buddhaghosa narrates independently and only at the end of each section does he refer to the corresponding part in the *Cullavagga*. Only in a few places does he weave parts of the *Cullavagga* directly into his narration. This can be traced clearly in detail.

The narration begins (4,6-5,17) with Buddha's death and reports how Mahākassapa, remembering Subhadda's alarming remarks and, realising his own responsibility as a bearer of the doctrine appointed by the Buddha, decides to summon the monks to a council. Then, the corresponding section of the *Cullavagga* (5,18-22) is referred to by the word *yathāha*. This section does not follow from the previous narration, but represents an independent, second report, which partly repeats what has already been said. So, we are not concerned here with a part of Buddhaghosa's narration but actually with just a reference. The narration is then continued with a few sentences from the *Cullavagga* (6, 1-7). An independent report then follows about how Mahākassapa selects monks for the council, the considerations which lead him not to choose Ānanda for the moment, and how he, at the request of the other monks, finally selects him (6, 8-7, 19). In between a short reference to the choice of monks in the *Cullavagga* is inserted (6, 14f.) with the words *ye saṃdhāya idaṃ vuttaṃ* and, later, the words with which the monks request Mahākassapa to choose Ānanda are also taken from the *Cullavagga* (7, 12-18). Both these reports may be omitted without disturbing the continuity. Then, the narration is continued with a few sentences from the *Cullavagga* (7,20-8,4), and reference is made to the request which follows in the *Cullavagga*, which Mahākassapa puts to the monks (8,7f.). Thereafter, with a new entry an independent and detailed narration begins of Mahākassapa's and Anuruddha's journey to Rājagaha, of a visit to Sāvatthi by Ānanda, and of how the monks first repair the monasteries (8,9-9,26). The reference to the *Cullavagga* is briefly inserted with the words *vuttam pi c'etaṃ*, where the monks decide on the restoration work (10,1-5). The preparation for the council, which King Ajātasattu arranges at the request of the monks, is then described in detail (10,6-11,10). Then follows the narration of how Ānanda attains Arhathood even before the council (11,11-13,2). Here too the corresponding section of the *Cullavagga* is inserted (11,20-26). However, it could be omitted without any harm because immediately afterwards the same content is related, more in detail and partly with the same words (11,26-12,14). Even the report about the council begins at first with an independent narration of how, together with the monks, Mahākassapa decides to recite the Vinaya, under the guidance of Upāli (13,3-15). Then, with the words *tatrāyaṃ pāli*, follows the corresponding place of the *Cullavagga* (13,16-21) which, in a somewhat different form, also relates how it was decided to consult Upāli about the Vinaya. If one omits this then the sentences which follow flow from the preceding report without a break (13,21-24). Only the consultation with Upāli follows the *Cullavagga* verbatim (13, 25-14,7), but the rest of the report about the compilation of the Vinaya is again independent (14,7-15,11). The report about the compilation of the Dhamma is very similar. In the introductory, independent presentation (15,12-23) the corresponding part of the *Cullavagga* is again inserted (15,16-21) which, however, can be omitted without creating a vacuum. Then, the questions to Ānanda follow the words of the *Cullavagga* (15,23-16,12). The conclusion is again independent. With this the actual report about the council ends. Then follow long descriptions about the compilation of the canon (16,18-30,5). With a few independent sentences, the report is finally concluded (30,6-14).

We thus have the following findings: the report in the *Cullavagga* does not constitute the core of Buddhaghosa's presentation, but rather, a narration independent of it where pieces of the *Cullavagga* are interwoven only to a modest degree. In the rest, the corresponding sections of the *Cullavagga* are merely referred to. Thus, one cannot say that Buddhaghosa used the report in the *Cullavagga* as a basis and elaborated it using only the Aṭṭhakathā. Especially the places where sections from the *Cullavagga* are quoted, repeating only what has already been reported in the main narration (5, 18-22; 10, 1-5; 11, 20-26; 13, 16-21 and 15, 16-21) forbid such a view. On the contrary, we have, in the main, an independent narration in which there is an attempt to reconcile it with the authoritative, canonical presentation in the *Cullavagga*. If we ask where the independent narration came from, then it seems likely that it is taken from Buddhaghosa's source, the *Vinayaṭṭhakathā*. The link to the report in the *Cullavagga*, though, may hardly go back to the Aṭṭhakathā, because it is difficult to imagine a connection between the Pali text of the *Cullavagga* and the Singhalese narration of the Aṭṭhakathā. We may thus see as highly probable that this link is the work of Buddhaghosa.

This conclusion which one can draw from the report about the first council remains unchanged by the composition of the report about the second council. Here Buddhaghosa makes his task easier since he mainly refers only to the *Cullavagga* presentation (34, 9f.). Nonetheless, even here the introductory piece and the conclusion show a tendency towards an independent presentation. And it is to be pointed out especially that in the conclusion (34, 16ff.), over and above the presentation of the *Cullavagga* - though concurring with the Singhalese tradition - a recitation of the canon is reported after the decision over the contentious ten points.

Thus, we arrive at the conclusion that Buddhaghosa, for his report on the first two councils, largely follows the presentation in the Singhalese Aṭṭhakathā, about which we may get a fairly good picture in this way. It was a detailed narration which in some points differed from the canonical representation. Above all, it largely restricted itself to the main events which led to the collection of the canon at the first council. And this is quite natural since this section of the *Samantapāsādikā*, and with it also the Aṭṭhakathā, only wants to report about the tradition of the doctrine. The individual episodes which make up the conclusion of the *Cullavagga*, such as Ānanda's reprimand and Channa's punishment, are therefore omitted. Further, it is not related at the beginning how Mahākassapa learns of Buddha's death from an Ājīvaka monk and how the monks break out in lamentation. On the other hand, the main report, over and above the canonical presentation, is elaborated in detail. Even completely new particulars appear, like the grand preparation for the council by King Ajātasattu. Finally, Ānanda's strong prominence deserves special mention, his journey to Sāvatthi (8, 16-9,13), the detailed report about his attaining Arhathood (11, 11-13, 2) and, above all, that it is emphasized in the report about the council itself that Ānanda would have been capable even of reciting the Vinaya, and that Upāli was appointed to do it only because the Buddha had described him as the best bearer of the Vinaya.

Now that we have discussed the introduction to the *Samantapāsādikā* in so far as it deals with the first two councils, we may now turn to the remaining part. A canonical source is lacking here. Instead, one finds numerous quotations in it, in several of which the *Dīpavaṃsa* is explicitly mentioned as their source. And since the presentation of this section largely concurs with the *Dīpavaṃsa* the question can be raised whether it is indeed the source which Buddhaghosa follows here. On the other hand, however, it is obvious that one assumes the same conditions here as for the first part, namely, that here also Buddhaghosa essentially follows the presentation of *Vinayaṭṭhakathā*, and that he merely inserts references to most important other sources. In fact, even this assumption can be substantiated.

We have already spoken above (pp. 11ff) about quotations from the *Vinayaṭṭhakathā* contained in the *Vaṃsatthappakāsinī*. Without exception, these are taken from the part of the narration which constitute the second part of the introduction to the *Samantapāsādikā*. Thus, this was also represented in the *Vinayaṭṭhakathā*. One of these quotations is concerned with the Asoka legend, another with the history of the missions, and the remaining two are related to the events in Ceylon. Thus, the *Vinayaṭṭhakathā* presented the narration of this part completely. We saw, finally, that in three of these quotations the presentation of the *Vinayaṭṭhakathā* differed from that of the old *Mahāvaṃsa*. In all these cases Buddhaghosa follows the *Vinayaṭṭhakathā* over against the *Dīpavaṃsa* which represents the tradition of the *Mahāvaṃsa*. Thus, it may be regarded as proved that Buddaghosa's presentation in the second part of the introduction to the *Samantapāsādikā* is also linked to the *Vinayaṭṭhakathā*, and that the quotations from the *Dīpavaṃsa* are to be seen merely as references.

Thus, with Buddhaghosa's help we can obtain a picture also of this part of the Aṭṭhakathā. However, the question remains whether Buddhaghosa takes liberties with his source. And, indeed, we have to answer in the affirmative. First, we saw in the discussion about the quotations from the *Vinayaṭṭhakathā* that the determining of the borders of Tissārāma by King Devānampiyatissa is not narrated in the *Samantapāsādikā*, and one would have to assume that Buddhaghosa abridges his source at this point. On the other hand, the opposite also seems probable at other places. For example, the *Vaṃsatthappakāsinī* sometimes also quotes the *Samantapāsādikā*, in addition to the *Vinayaṭṭhakathā*. The first case (146, 20 = *Samantapāsādikā* 10, 19ff.) deals with a description of the magnificent hall which King Ajātasattu had built for the purpose of the first council; the second (239, 6 = *Samantapāsādikā* 57, 26ff.) with a detail about King Asoka's receiving Tissa Moggaliputta. It would not be understandable that the *Vaṃsatthappakāsinī* quotes the *Samantapāsādikā* here when the same could be found in the original source, namely the *Vinayaṭṭhakathā*. And since in both cases the presentation of the *Samantapāsādikā* is especially broad and detailed, the conclusion to be drawn is that Buddhaghosa goes beyond his source here and that he enlarged and embellished it. It is noteworthy in this context that the abridgement concerns details of interest only locally for Ceylon, namely drawing the border of Tissārāma, whereas both the enlargements concern the motherland; this leads to important conclusions for an evaluation of the Buddhaghosa legend. But this should be dealt with at another place (see Appendix I).[9] What is important for us here is that, despite faithfulness to the source in general, we have indeed to take into account abridgements and enlargements by Buddhaghosa.

Thus, the first part of our investigation is completed. It has shown that the *Vinayaṭṭhakathā* of Mahāvihāra in Singhalese was the source of the introduction to Buddhaghosa's *Samantapāsādikā*. As for the composition of this source, we saw that Buddhaghosa generally presents it faithfully. He strives only to reconcile it with the appropriate, authoritative Pāli sources of his time, insofar as he refers to the presentation in the *Cullavagga* for his report of the first two councils and to the *Dīpavaṃsa* for the rest of the narration. But, we also have to reckon with occasional abridgement or enlargement of his source.

## 2. The Source of the Dīpavaṃsa and Mahāvaṃsa

We turn next to the question about the source of the *Dīpavaṃsa* and the *Mahāvaṃsa*. But first we have to deal with a minor preliminary question. It is accepted that both works go back to the same source, since the agreement in content and structure make any doubt impossible. However, their relation to each other is uncertain. The *Dīpavaṃsa* is the older work. The *Mahāvaṃsa* is later and knows of the *Dīpavaṃsa.* The question now is whether the *Mahāvaṃsa* presents a mere revision of the *Dīpavaṃsa*, or whether it independently utilizes the common source.

The old commentary to the *Mahāvaṃsa*, the *Vaṃsatthappakāsinī*, assumes that it draws from the basic work itself.[10] This is not decisive for us. The *Vaṃsatthappakāsinī* is at least a hundred and fifty years later than the *Mahāvaṃsa* and is, therefore, hardly based on a

---

9 [Not supplied].

10 It is stated there explicitly several times, that the *Mahāvaṃsa* is an adaption of the *Sīhalaṭṭhakathāmahāvaṃsa*, with only the language changed, but the content being essentially retained (e.g., 48, 3ff.; 687, 3ff.; c/f. W. Geiger, loc.cit., pp. 47f.). The same view seems to have been already held by the older commentator Pasanadīpavāsī Upatissathera (47, 25ff.).

direct tradition, but rather, rests only on the far-reaching agreement of the *Mahāvaṃsa* with the basic work. What is more important is that the *Mahāvaṃsa* recorded some things from the basic text which go beyond the *Dīpavaṃsa*. If it represents a revision of the *Dīpavaṃsa*, it is of course possible that it, in addition, draws from the basic work. However, on the other hand, the numerous concurrences with the *Dīpavaṃsa* do not prove that it is a mere revision of this work; because it is just as well imaginable that in revising the basic work, it also used the already existing *Dīpavaṃsa*. So it is not easy to decide. I would, nonetheless, like to express the view that in the *Mahāvaṃsa* we see a revision of the *Dīpavaṃsa* for the following reasons.

Above all, in my view, the similar scope of both these works speak in favour of it, namely, that both conclude with the reign of King Mahāsena, whereas with an independent work, it would be natural that the later work would continue the report. Some tried to explain this (W. Geiger, loc.cit., 71) by the point that under Mahāsena Mahāvihāra was destroyed and that its chronicle was not continued. But this can hardly be correct. We know from the *Cūlavaṃsa* (XXXVII, v. 54-64) that Mahāsena's successor, his son Sirimeghavaṇṇa, had already reinstated Mahāvihāra. And a few decades later, during Buddhaghosa's time, it flourished again. The blow was thus overcome quickly. Moreover, the manuscripts of the monastery were not destroyed. Buddhaghosa, Mahānāma, and even the author of the *Vaṃsatthappakāsinī* know about them and use them. So this explanation is erroneous. On the other hand, the situation is completely understandable if we consider the *Mahāvaṃsa* to be a revision of the *Dīpavaṃsa*. The *Dīpavaṃsa*, which even Buddhaghosa quotes, was apparently written during the reign of Mahāsena, or soon afterwards and, thus, furnishes a description of events upto his time. And the *Mahāvaṃsa*, as a revision of the *Dīpavaṃsa*, naturally ends where its source breaks off.

### 3. The Composition and Structure of the Old Mahāvaṃsa

We have attempted thus far in our task to determine the sources of the works in question and came to the conclusion that Buddhaghosa's presentation in the *Samantapāsādikā* is based on the *Vinayaṭṭhakathā* of Mahāvihāra which in general is given faithfully, whereas the *Dīpavaṃsa* and the *Mahāvaṃsa* rest on the old *Mahāvaṃsa*, an independent work which consisted of a short basic text, largely in verse, and an extensive commentary. Our next task is now to analyse these sources, as far as they may be comprehended through the later revisions. Thus, we shall attempt to determine the parts out of which they have been composed, where these parts came from and how the works at hand evolve out of them.

For this investigation I shall begin with the more extensive of the two mentioned sources, namely, with the old *Mahāvaṃsa*. Of the two works derived from it I shall use, in the first place, the *Dīpavaṃsa* as a basis for the following reasons. First, the *Dīpavaṃsa* is the older work and the model for the *Mahāvaṃsa*. Second, we saw that the *Dīpavaṃsa* essentially reproduces the basic work, whereas the *Mahāvaṃsa* inserts various, often later, additions from the commentary and partly also from other sources. Finally, because the *Dīpavaṃsa* is the lesser independent work. For an analysis of a source a work is more valuable the more the author is restricted by his source, i.e., the less he changes the material which he takes over and builds into his own work. On the other hand, precisely with a significant writer who penetrates the material and shapes it in his own way, an analysis of its source becomes difficult and sometimes almost impossible. In this sense the *Dīpavaṃsa* provides an almost ideal basis because, whereas in his *Mahāvaṃsa* Mahānāma strives to present the material in a well-balanced way and to produce a continuous narration, the author of the *Dīpavaṃsa*, on the other hand, strings the parts of his source together and does not even attempt to conceal the gaps.

Before we attempt to separate these parts we need to discuss a striking phenomenon. It has been noticed quite early that some parts in the *Dīpavaṃsa* recur several times. At first Geiger wanted to see in it the reflection of an originally oral tradition, assuming thereby that the variations of the oral tradition would be maintained (loc.cit., 10f.). However, he gradually realized "that it indeed was not a matter of mere 'repetition' ... but also, in fact, often a matter of two versions of the same narration" and that, possibly, "the compiler of the Dīpavaṃsa, in addition to the *Aṭṭhakathāmahāvaṃsa* of Mahāvihāra, on which Mahānāma's work is based, used still another source work" (loc.cit., 76). This view is now the only correct one. A closer investigation reveals that there is nowhere a question of several versions, as Geiger thought, but rather that there have always been only two versions whose individual pieces are connected to each other through several features, whilst being distiguished from each other by characteristic traits. Only once does a third version appear, but this case too has a satisfactory explanation (see below, p. 23).

I am first presenting an outline of the sections appearing in the two versions respectively, where A refers to the the first version and B to the second without, for the present, wanting to say anything about their connections.

| Version A | | Version B |
|---|---|---|
| IV, v. 1-26 | 1st Council | V, v. 1-14 |
| IV, v. 27-46<br>V, v. 69-75<br>v. 89-94 | List of Patriarchs | V, v. 76-82;<br>v. 95-102;<br>v. 103-107 |
| IV, v. 47-53 | 2nd Council | V, v. 15-29 (30-54) |
| VII, v. 34-43 | 3rd Council | VII, v. 44-59 |
| XI, v. 32-40 | Asoka's message to Devānampiyatissa | XII, v. 1-7 |
| XII, v. 16-28 +<br>v. 36f. | Mahinda's arrival in Ceylon | XII, v. 29-35+<br>v. 38-41 |
| XV, v. 34-73 | The 4 Buddhas in Ceylon | XVII, v. 1-74 |
| XIX, v. 1-22 | The Kings from Duṭṭhagāmani upto Mahātissa | XIX, v. 23-XX, v. 23 |
| XXII, v. 12-26 | The Kings of Vaṅkanāsikatissa upto Kuñjanāga | XXII, v. 27-33 |

As this first outline shows, the sections are from various parts of the work. The *Dīpavaṃsa*, now, used two source works with about the same scope and content and so we should not in fact speak of two source works but, rather, of two versions of a single basic work, namely the old *Mahāvaṃsa*, which were accessible to the writer of the *Dīpavaṃsa*, both of which he used whenever they seemed appropriate to him.

What is the situation regarding these two versions? According to the *Vaṃsatthappakāsinī* the main source of the *Mahāvaṃsa*, and with it also that of the *Dīpavaṃsa*, was the old *Mahāvaṃsa* of Mahāvihāra, i.e., a chronicle of a specific monastery. Thus, it seems possible to see in the second version a chronicle of another monastery. Now, the *Vaṃsatthappakāsinī*, in fact, knows about a second, similar work which it quotes several times,[11] in addition to the *Mahāvaṃsa* of Mahā-

[11] C/f. W. Geiger, loc.cit., 52 and Malalasekera, loc.cit., LXV ff.

vihāra. As it appears from the quotations, even this work contained a short basic text and a detailed commentary, and Geiger has shown that, to a very large extent, even the content covers the *Mahāvaṃsa* of Mahāvihāra.[12] This second work is the *Mahāvaṃsa* of Uttaravihāra. It is very likely that it is the second source of the *Dīpavaṃsa*. However, there is no direct evidence since the quotations in the *Vaṃsatthappakāsinī* do not come from any of the sections which have come down to us in both versions. Nonetheless, it seems so highly probable to me that I would like to use it as a working hypothesis. Uttaravihāra, to which the second version of the old *Mahāvaṃsa* belongs, is in all probability the famous Abhayagirivihāra in the north of Anurādhapura.[13] In general, however, there is no talk of a Uttaravihāra in the old chronicles but, in the *Cūlavaṃsa*, Abhayagirivihāra is very often referred to as Abhayuttaravihāra[14] and even called simply Uttaravihāra in some places.[15] Therefore, the identification seems justified.

The existence of two versions is of great significance, since it enables us at least to take a fleeting glance at the tradition of the rival, neighbour monastery - in addition to the relatively better known tradition of Mahāvihāra; its importance will be evident when we investigate and evaluate the tradition regarding its origin. First, however, in order to obtain a general overview, it is better not to consider the repetitions since they only contribute to veiling the simple and clear structure of the work.

If we look at the *Dīpavaṃsa* as a whole, it is clearly divided into four parts. After a few introductory verses it begins with a report of the Buddha's three visits to Ceylon, which extends over the first two chapters. Then the third chapter follows without any transition, enumerating the kings of the present age, going back to the Buddha and his contemporaries. Both sections represent a kind of past history. However, they have nothing to do with each other as far as the content is concerned, and each is rather a self-contained unit. They are different from each other even from the point of view of their origins. The legend of

---

[12] W. Geiger, loc.cit., 54ff.

[13] This also seems to be the view of Malalasekera, c/f. loc. cit., LXVff. Geiger does not deal with the question at all.

[14] E.g., *Cūlavaṃsa* XXXVII, v. 97 (and Geiger's note to it in his translation), v. 212; XXXVIII, v. 61; XLI, v. 31, etc.

[15] *Cūlavaṃsa* XLI, v. 96.

Buddha's visits to Ceylon was of interest only in Ceylon and was thus created there, whereas the list of kings, the *Rājavaṃśaḥ*, is based on the tradition of the motherland. We may therefore view both these sections as originally independent parts of the *Dīpavaṃsa*, or of its source, the older *Mahāvaṃsa*.

Then in Chapters IV-XXII a history of the church follows in great detail. It begins with the first two councils and with a list of the patriarchs, then goes into the reign of Asoka, tells of his conversion, of the third council and of the dispatch of various missionaries (IV-VIII). Then the narration goes back to the colonization of Ceylon and gives a history of the island upto King Devānampiyatissa, the contemporary of Asoka (IX-XI, v. 14). Then follows a detailed report on the conversion of Ceylon, the arrival of the messengers of the faith, the conversion of King Devānampiyatissa, the founding of the first monasteries, the construction of the first stūpas, the planting of a branch of the holy Bodhi tree and the founding of the Ceylonese church by ordinating local monks and nuns (XI, v. 15-XVII, v. 74). Then a history of Ceylon follows, up until King Mahāsena, i.e., upto the time when the *Dīpavaṃsa* was composed (XVII, v. 75-XXII, v. 76).

The entire report constitutes a single unit as far as the content is concerned, but is nonetheless clearly made up of two parts: the actual history of the church and a chronicle of Ceylon. The difference in the two parts is striking. The history of the church furnishes a detailed, continuous narration. The chronicle gives a dry enumeration of the Ceylonese kings, with short statements about their religious deeds. Besides, the two parts are put together unconnectedly and an attempt is not even made to conceal the gaps. With the end of the eighth chapter the church history ceases and then suddenly the chronicle, going as far as the reign of Muṭasīva, begins (XI, v. 5). After enumerating the children of Muṭasīva and after making a few chronological observations (v. 6-14), it continues with the church history and narrates in a continuous way the history of the conversion of Ceylon (XI, v. 15-XVII, v. 74). Following this, and without any transition, the chronicle is once again taken up and continues upto Mahāsena (XVII, v. 75-XXII, v. 76), and only once more interrupted by a detailed report on the death and funeral of the apostle of Ceylon, Mahinda, and an enumeration of the important monks and nuns of Ceylon (XVII, v. 95-XVIII, v. 44). Even here, the transition is abrupt and sudden (especially XVIII, v. 45).

The clearest evidence that we are here dealing with two originally independent works is, however, the following. After the history of Ceylon's conversion the chronicle once again inserted the enumeration of the children of Muṭasīva (XVII, v. 75ff.), and then the coronation of Devānampiyatissa, his conversion, and his religious institutions are again reported, namely, everything that was already narrated fully and in detail, but now in a short, dry chronicle style. Here it cannot be related to a second version, as would otherwise be the case, because the beginning of the report with Asoka's message had already been given in two versions (XI, v. 32-40 = XII, v. 1-7). So, there may have been a third version. But the completely different form of the presentation indicates that this is not the case. We have here, rather, the report of the chronicle about the same events, as opposed to the earlier report of the church history. Thus, both the church history and the chronicle have narrated the same events independently of each other, and this is understandable only if they were originally independent works. At the same time, one can explain in this way the single case where three versions appear in the *Dīpavaṃsa* (see above, pp. 20f.).

On the other hand, both these works, the church history and the chronicle, each make up a unit in itself. In the chronicle the flowing continuity and similarity of the presentation is obvious. Even the church history, in the form in which we have it, represents a planned unity. This can be seen in the dovetailing which bind the individual parts together. Thus, after the second council, the third is predicted (V, v. 55-60), and its chief figure, Moggaliputta, is introduced by way of a narration of his youth (V, v. 61-68). In the history of Asoka, which is inserted between the second and third councils, first the origin (VI, v. 15-17) and later the consecration (VII, v. 18-33) of Mahinda, the apostle of Ceylon, is narrated, and, in this way, his later appearance is prepared for, etc. Above all, however, this church history is still extant independently. The historical introduction in Buddhaghosa's *Samantapāsādikā* which, as we saw, comes from the old *Vinayaṭṭhakathā*, agrees, apart from insignificant particulars, with the scope and structure of the church history incorporated in the *Dīpavaṃsa* so exactly, that we have to regard both as a single work which is extant here and there in two different versions.

With regard to the construction of the *Dīpavaṃsa*, and with it its source, the old *Mahāvaṃsa*, we have for the moment the following results.[16] The old *Mahāvaṃsa* consisted of several, originally independent parts and, in fact, four such parts can be distinguished:

1. A report on Buddha's visits to Ceylon;
2. A *Rājavaṃśaḥ*, i.e., a list of the kings of this age upto the time of Buddha;
3. A church history, beginning with the first council and concluding with an enumeration of the important monks and nuns of Ceylon; and
4. A chronicle of Ceylon, from the colonization of the island upto Mahāsena.

Our next task now is to consider these parts with regard to their origin, formation and significance, and we shall begin with the most detailed part, namely, the church history.

## 4. The Church History

I would like to present first an overview of the contents of the church history. As we saw, we have it in two traditions, in the presentation in the *Samantapāsādikā*, which is based on the *Vinayaṭṭhakathā*, and in the presentation in the *Dīpavaṃsa*, which reiterates the old *Mahāvaṃsa* of Mahāvihāra. Where the *Dīpavaṃsa* also records the version of Uttaravihāra in addition to that of Mahāvihāra, we can take a third tradition into consideration. In what follows I am supplying the content of each section in themes, together with their occurrence in each of the versions.[17]

| | A | | B | Smp |
|---|---|---|---|---|
| 1. First Council | IV, v. 1-26 | | V, v. 1-14 | 4,6-30,14 |
| 2. List of Patriarchs | IV, v. 27-46 | | — | 31,25-33,6 |
| 3. Second Council | IV, v. 47-53 | | V, v. 15-29 | 33,7-35-7 |
| 4. Mahāsaṃgīti; Origin of the various schools | — | | V, v. 30-54 | — |
| 5. Prediction of Third Council | | V, v. 55-60 | | 35,8-37,6 |

16 [C/f. Appendix B].

17 Here too A refers to the first version of the *Dīpavaṃsa* and B to the second. If there is only one version, I supply the reference in the middle. Smp = *Samantapāsādikā*. I am quoting the *Dīpavaṃsa* according to chapter and verse numbers, the *Samantapāsādikā* according to page and line numbers.

<table>
<tr><th></th><th>A</th><th>B</th><th>Smp</th></tr>
<tr><td>6. Mogaliputta's youth</td><td colspan="2">V, v. 61-68</td><td>37,7-41.20</td></tr>
<tr><td>7. List of Patriarchs</td><td>V, v. 69-75;<br>v. 89-94</td><td>V, v. 76-82;<br>v. 95-107</td><td>—</td></tr>
<tr><td>8. Asoka as Cakravartin</td><td colspan="2">VI, 1-12</td><td>41,21-43,7</td></tr>
<tr><td>9. Nāga Kāla</td><td colspan="2">VI, v. 13f.</td><td>43,8-44,5</td></tr>
<tr><td>10. Mahinda's birth</td><td colspan="2">VI, v. 15-17</td><td>—</td></tr>
<tr><td>11. Asoka's conversion by Nigrodha</td><td colspan="2">VI, v. 18; v. 24-56</td><td>44,6-48,18</td></tr>
<tr><td>12. (Nigrodha's youth)</td><td colspan="2">—</td><td>45,7-46,10</td></tr>
<tr><td>13. (Asoka's, Nigrodha's and Tissa's contact in an earlier birth)</td><td colspan="2">—</td><td>46,23-47,2</td></tr>
<tr><td>14. Asoka's invitation of the order; founding of 84,000 cloisters</td><td colspan="2">VI, v. 57-99</td><td>48,19-49,16</td></tr>
<tr><td>15. Celebration of completion of building; Mahinda and Saṃghamittā enter the order</td><td colspan="2">VII, v. 1-31</td><td>49,17-52,10</td></tr>
<tr><td>16. Tissa's and Sumitta's death lead to establishing medicine stocks</td><td colspan="2">VII, v. 32f.</td><td>52,10-19</td></tr>
<tr><td>17. Third Council</td><td>VII, v. 34-43</td><td>VII, v. 44-59</td><td>52,20-61,25</td></tr>
<tr><td>18. Dispatch of numerous missionaries</td><td colspan="2">VIII</td><td>63,20-69,15</td></tr>
<tr><td>19. Date of Ceylon's conversion; lists of kings</td><td colspan="2">XI, v. 8-14</td><td>72, 5-73,11</td></tr>
<tr><td>20. Devānampiyatissa's and Asoka's friendship</td><td colspan="2">XI, v. 15-31</td><td>74, 7-75,6</td></tr>
<tr><td>21. Asoka's message to Devānampiyatissa</td><td>XI, v. 32-40</td><td>XII, v. 1-7</td><td>75,6-76,14</td></tr>
<tr><td>22. Mahinda's stay in Vedissa</td><td colspan="2">XII, v .7-15</td><td>69,16-70,20</td></tr>
<tr><td>23. His flight to Ceylon</td><td>XII, v. 16-28;<br>v. 36f.</td><td>XII, v. 29-35;<br>v. 38-41</td><td>70,20-72,4</td></tr>
<tr><td>24. Devānampiyatissa's meeting with Mahinda</td><td colspan="2">XII, v. 45-63</td><td>73,12-74,6;<br>76,14-78,11</td></tr>
<tr><td>25. Announcing hour of sermon</td><td colspan="2">—</td><td>78,12-79,3</td></tr>
<tr><td>26. First sermon; night in Mahāmeghavana</td><td colspan="2">XII, v. 64-XIII, v. 25</td><td>79,4-81,14</td></tr>
<tr><td>27. King donates Mahāmeghavana to the order</td><td colspan="2">XIII, v. 26-37</td><td>81,14-25</td></tr>
<tr><td>28. Mahinda decides the places for cloisters</td><td colspan="2">XIII, v. 38-XIV, v. 7</td><td>—</td></tr>
<tr><td>29. Additional sermons</td><td colspan="2">XIV, v. 8-19</td><td>81,25-82,2</td></tr>
<tr><td>30. Setting of Tissārāma border</td><td colspan="2">XIV, v. 20-40</td><td>—</td></tr>
<tr><td>31. Additional sermons</td><td colspan="2">XIV, v. 40-49</td><td>—</td></tr>
</table>

| | A | B | Smp |
|---|---|---|---|
| 32. Mahinda spends rainy season on Missaka mountain; King establishes cloister there; Mahāariṭṭha becomes monk | XIV, v. 50-80 | | 82,3-83,4 |
| 33. Building the first stūpa | XV, v. 1-33 | | 83,5-90,13 |
| 34. The four Buddhas in Ceylon | XV, v. 34-73 | | 86,7-87,23; (89, 10-21) |
| 35. Planting of Bodhitree; Anulā becomes nun | XV, v. 74-XVI, v. 41 | | 90,14-101,6 |
| 36. The four Buddhas in Ceylon | XVII, v. 1-74 | | — |
| 37. Mahinda decides places for buildings in Thūpārāma | — | | 101,7-102,7 |
| 38. Founding of local Ceylonese church | — | | 102,8-104,6 |
| 39. Mahinda's death and funeral | XVII, v. 95-109 | | — |
| 40. Important monks and nuns of Ceylon | XVIII, v. 1-44 | | 104,7-11 (62,8-63,18) |

A look at the above plan gives a picture of general agreement to a large extent. The differences between the two versions of the old *Mahāvaṃsa* are minimal, as far as can be judged from the available material. One may only note the breaking up of the lists of patriarchs (nos. 2 and 7), and that one finds the first report about the four Buddhas in Ceylon (no. 34) inserted after the building of the first stūpa, and the second (no. 36) after the planting of the Bodhi tree.

Somewhat greater, but still not very significant, are the differences between the old *Mahāvaṃsa* and the *Samantapāsādikā*. We find several times additions in a text, but we need not consider all these cases. Thus, for example, neither does Nigrodha's youth (no. 12) appear in the old *Mahāvaṃsa*, nor the narration why Asoka, Nigrodha and Tissa were already in contact in an earlier existence (no.13), nor even the report announcing the hour of the sermon (no. 25). However, we may gather from Mahānāma's *Mahāvaṃsa* that these sections were to be found in the Aṭṭhakathā of the *Mahāvaṃsa* and that they lacked only in the basic text. And, in fact, at least the first two are also in the *Samantapāsādikā*, made evident as supplements by the way in which they are introduced. It is more significant that the report about Mahinda's birth and death (nos. 10 and 39) and the report about the origin of the Buddhist sects (no. 4) do not appear in the *Samantapāsādi-*

*kā*. As far as the arrangement of the contents is concerned, one notices two major deviations. The first is over the report about the friendship between Asoka and Devānampiyatissa, which in the old *Mahāvaṃsa* introduces the history of the conversion of Ceylon (nos. 19-21). Besides, the narration about Mahinda's decision regarding the places of the different buildings of the monastery in Tissārāma (no. 37) does not appear, as in the old *Mahāvaṃsa* (no. 28) after the donation of Mahāmeghavana, but rather, after the planting of the Bodhi tree. And the report on drawing the border (no. 30) is omitted totally.[18]

These are the essential differences. They are, as stated, minimal and the agreements definitely outweigh them. We can therefore say that an essentially similar form of the church history is evident in the extant versions, which in all probability goes back to quite old times.

The question we may now consider is whether the church history in this form represents a homogeneous new composition, or whether its author used older material, which can be traced back even earlier. At the outset, the recording of the report about the first two councils, which already appears in the canonical tradition of the *Vinayapiṭakam*, speaks for the use of older material. Even otherwise, this can be largely verified. After the first two councils there is a long narration which begins with Asoka's coronation and leads into the history of the conversion of Ceylon. It is held together by the person of Asoka. Its beginning constitutes a depiction of Asoka's wondrous powers as a Cakravartin. Then the story of his conversion follows, the building of the 84,000 cloisters, the entry of his children into the order, the holding of the third council under his patronage and cooperation. And, finally, it is his friendship with Devānampiyatissa which leads to the conversion of Ceylon. Despite this apparent continuity, it can nonetheless be shown that this report is composed of several parts which are only superficially connected to each other. Characteristic for it is, above all, that for each of these parts a different monk appears as the dominant personality, namely, Nigrodha in the early history, Moggaliputta at the third council, and Mahinda in the history of Ceylon's conversion. Each person is omitted in the respective remaining parts, or if the person appears individually then one can easily recognize that he is introduced secondarily.

---

[18] As we already saw above (p. 11), it was first omitted by Buddhaghosa.

Moggaliputta's case is especially instructive. He first appears at Mahinda's initiation (D VII, v. 16ff.). On the other hand, the *Samantapāsādikā* (56,16ff.) in the report on the third council and Mahānāma's *Mahāvaṃsa* (V, v. 245ff.), which reports in much more detail than the *Dīpavaṃsa*, narrates that Asoka sought a teacher who could resolve his doubts and clarify the doctrine, and that, accordingly, Moggaliputta is named, that he is ceremoniously appointed and installed. All this is absurd if he was already in contact with Asoka beforehand and had initiated his son as a monk. So, Moggaliputta must have originally appeared in the report on the third council for the first time. And since he is here the chief person who could not be ignored, whereas he plays merely a secondary role at Mahinda's initiation, we have to conclude that he originally belonged to the history of the third council and was only secondarily brought in contact with Mahinda.[19]

But just as Moggaliputta first appears in the report on the third council, so too does he disappear after the council. He is last mentioned together with the dispatching of missionaries immediately after the council (D VIII, v. 1). Mahinda never mentions him as his teacher, and in his communications he turns directly to Asoka and not to Moggaliputta (D XV, v. 6ff., and v. 88ff.), even though, according to the chronological details (D V, v.94), he lived a further twenty six years after Mahinda's initiation.

With that the person Moggaliputta is removed from the rest of the narration and, especially, from the story of Mahinda, and with him the event of which he was the chief bearer, namely, the third council, is removed from this context. The report about the third council actually appears in both versions of the *Dīpavaṃsa* as a self-contained unit, so that such a removal is possible without any difficulty. And, besides, the assumption that he was originally separated from the story about

[19] His appearance at Mahinda's initiation cannot be explained as a mere error in the order of the narration. The despatching of missionaries immediately after the council (D VIII, v. 1ff.) presupposes Mahinda's initiation. And even in the chronological statement this sequence is established. Mahinda's initiation took place six years after Asoka's coronation (D VII, v. 31), i.e., in 224 after Nirvana, the council in 236 a. N. (D VII, v. 44). Furthermore, it would not be improper to assume that Moggaliputta was made Mahinda's teacher only later. It is, in fact, the rule that the narratives of the youth of such favourite figures of legends, like that of Mahinda, are secondary inventions. And here it was only natural to make Moggaliputta, the famous head of the school, his teacher. But we shall return to this later. [This was not completed; c/f. Appendix A].

Mahinda is obvious, since it is based on reports from various sources. The report on the third council, in fact, belongs to the church history of the motherland and has certainly originated there. On the other hand, the story about Mahinda, which is essentially the history of the conversion of Ceylon, evinces such a knowledge of the place and is so full of details which were of interest only in Ceylon, that we may assume a Ceylonese origin with certainty. We would then be led to the assumption that the church history in the *Mahāvaṃsa* is in fact composed of two parts, having different sources: the church history of the motherland and the history of the conversion of Ceylon, the first of which has its origin in the motherland and the second in Ceylon. The report on the three councils belongs, in the first place, to the church history of the motherland, whereas the history of Ceylon's conversion would cover, above all, the lengthy, continuous report from Devānampiyatissa's ascension to the throne, to Mahinda's death.

However, what speaks against this assumption is the fact that the history of the missions (no. 18) in the traditional form of the church history, is closely connected to the third council, and that it was initiated by Moggaliputta. This is the case only at first glance. A closer investigation makes evident, rather, that precisely this report on the missions speaks strongly in favour of a division of the church history into a part of the motherland and into a Ceylonese part. The presentation runs as follows. It is reported, first, how Moggaliputta sends out several missions immediately after the third council. Then the narration begins anew and describes Devānampiyatissa's coronation, his message to Asoka, this one's call for conversion and, finally, Mahinda's journey to Ceylon. These are in reality two different reports which are put one after the other here. And that this is in fact so, evince not only the report in the narration and the completely new beginning, but, moreso, the various attempts to conceal this break. At first it was thought necessary to justify the point that Mahinda did not commence his journey immediately after the end of the third council, like the other missionaries did, but that he postponed it, until Devānampiyatissa's message and Asoka's answer urge him to it. It is reported (no. 22) that Mahinda first went to Vedissa to his mother and remained there a long time because, according to the *Samantapāsādikā* (69, 16ff.), he realized that the old King Mūṭasiva was not the right man to receive and to propagate the doctrine, and because he wanted to wait for the ascension to the throne of the new King Devānampiyatissa. This is, of course, a typical legendary tradition without any historical value. However, with this very justification the break in the narration remained all the more glaring and odd, so that it was attempted to eliminate it in various ways. Immediately after the report on the dispatch of the missions (no. 18), the *Samantapāsādikā* narrates the story of Mahinda (nos. 22-23) and makes up only afterwards for the narration of Devānampiyatissa's and Asoka's friendship and Asoka's message (nos. 19-21). This is one of the few cases, as we saw (p. 27), in which the presentation in the *Samantapāsādikā*, deviates from that of the *Mahāvaṃsa*. The case is similar with Mahānāma's *Mahāvaṃsa*, which is different in only two instances in the order of the material of the *Dīpavaṃsa* (see W. Geiger, *Dīpavaṃsa und Mahāvaṃsa*, 14f.), and one of these instances is that it puts the entire report about the missions (nos. 18, 22, and 23) after Asoka's message (no. 21). And this is also an attempt to avoid the break in the continuity and to try and provide a harmonious sequence in the narration.

How can one now explain this duality in the report and the consequent break in the narration? The answer is provided by the composition of the reports themselves. In the first (no. 18) the initiative for the missions comes from Moggaliputta. Quite a number of missions are involved, and the mission to Ceylon is in no way given any preference, but is summarily mentioned and done with as one of the others. In the second report (no. 19ff.) it is the diplomatic correspondence between the two Kings Devānampiyatissa and Asoka, and Asoka's personal initiative, which is responsible for Mahinda's dispatch. There is, however, no mention of any other missions. Instead, the sequence of Mahinda's undertaking is described in all its details. This difference is immediately understandable no sooner we assume that the first report comes from the church history of the motherland, whereas the second is based on the Ceylonese tradition. It is obvious that the church of the motherland should ascribe the dispatching of the mission to Moggaliputta, the famous head of the school. All the missions were important for it and so the mission to Ceylon had to appear as one of the others. In Ceylon, however, there was little concern about Moggaliputta and the other missions. On the other hand, King Devānampiyatissa was known, under whom the conversion to Buddhism ensued, and it is quite posssible that the report about his contact with Asoka has historical reminiscences in it. And it was natural here to commit to memory even the most important event for the religious history of the country, namely, the conversion to Buddhism, in full sequence, and described and elaborated in all details. With this point our original assumption is confirmed and, at the same time, the reason not only for the report on the missions appearing directly after the third council, but also the break that is caused through it, is explained.

Thus, we have to distinguish two components, which are also different as far as their sources are concerned, in the church history of the old *Mahāvaṃsa* and the *Samantapāsādikā*: one is a church history of the motherland which covers the period from Buddha's death upto the third council and the dispatch of the missions (nos. 1-7 and 17-18), and the other, a detailed history of Ceylon's conversion (nos. 19-40). The first presents, upto a point, the past history of Ceylon's church, it accounts for the origin and tradition of the sacred doctrine and naturally breaks off where, with the conversion, the local church history of Ceylon is inserted. It is based on the reports of the motherland which came to Ceylon through the missions. The second component deals with the founding of the local Ceylonese national church and is based on Ceylonese sources.

We have not yet placed in proper context the section which contains the history of Asoka upto the third council (nos. 8-16). It is a coherent narration and reports, in increasing intensity, Asoka's ascension to the throne, his conversion, his religious foundations and, finally, the entry of his children into the order. Mahinda's initiation is also a climax towards which the narration strives. And I therefore think that this entire section is meant to be Mahinda's past history and is, as such, recorded in the entire presentation. The evidence for this, as well as the answer to the question about the composition of this report and its sources, has to be provided by a detailed investigation of various sections of the text, to which we may now turn.

## 5. The Church History of the Motherland

The report on the three councils constitutes the core of the church history of the motherland. One knows about the first two of these councils from the tradition of the other schools as well. We learn of the third council only through the Ceylonese tradition. And there is a good reason for this. The missionizing of Ceylon began at a time when the Buddhist church was already split into several schools. Therefore the resources of the tradition, which reached Ceylon through the missionaries, encompasses not only components which belong to the oldest tradition common to all the schools, but also elements of the tradition of the parent order, out of which the mission emerged.

I have dealt with the councils themselves elsewhere,[20] and can therefore be brief here. The first two councils took place before the split of the original order. The first council goes back to the legendary time of the origin of the Buddhist church. It is separated by such a vast time span from the reports about it which are available to us, that one can understand from the reports merely how the composition of the canon of sacred writings was conceived of later, whereas it is difficult to extract anything historical out of them. On the other hand, the report on the second council can be regarded as old in relation to the reported events. It may, therefore, not only be historical for the fact of the council, but, also, some of the reported details appear to preserve true recollections.[21]

The split in the Buddhist church occurred after the second council. The conflict which led to the division followed a council in Pāṭaliputra in the second century after Nirvāṇa. The cause for it were the five theses, generally ascribed to Mahādeva. In the course of further conflicts the various schools were then formed. Their formation usually took place in a local synod at which the sacred writings were determined in a form recognized by the respective schools, under the leadership of an eminent teacher who took on the role of the head of the school. We are given an idea of these occurrences in the extant presentation of the Vātsīputrīya-Sāṃmitīya in Bhāvaviveka's *Tarkajvālā* about the formation of this school.[22] Thereafter the first conflict took place at the Pāṭaliputra council in the year 137 after Nirvāṇa. After a further 63 years, during which the quarrels continued, the eldest Vatsīputra arranged a compilation of the sacred writings in its proper form and, thereby, founded the Vātsīputrīya School. In a similar way, we can imagine the events in the parent order, from which the missionizing of Ceylon ensued and which I call the Pāli School. And, actually, the socalled third council of the Ceylonese tradition is to be regarded as a founding synod of this school with Tissa Moggaliputta as its head.

---

20 "Die buddhistischen Konzile", ZDMG 102, 1952, 240-261.

21 Otherwise it would be difficult to understand how a mere fiction could have spread and been given recognition in such a short time.

22 C/f. M. Walleser: *Die Sekten des alten Buddhismus,* Heidelberg, 1927, 81f.

**Literature**

Geiger W. (ed.): *Cūlavaṃsa, being the more recent part of the Mahāvaṃsa*, London: Vol. I 1925, Vol. II 1927.

Geiger W. (tr.): *Cūlavaṃsa, being the more recent part of the Mahāvaṃsa*, London: Vol. I 1929, Vol. II 1930.

Oldenberg, Hermann (ed. and tr.): *The Dīpavaṃsa: An Ancient Buddhist Historical Record*, London, 1879 [=D].

Geiger, Wilhelm (ed.): *The Mahāvaṃsa*, London, 1908.

Geiger, Wilhelm (tr.): *The Mahāvaṃsa or the Great Chronical of Ceylon*, London, 1912.

Takakusu J. and Nagai M. (eds.): *Samantapāsādikā, Buddhaghosa's Commentary on the Vinaya Piṭaka*, London, Vol. I, 1924 [= Smp].

Malalasekera G.P. (ed.) *Vaṃsatthappakāsinī Commentary on the Mahāvaṃsa, Vols. I, II*, London, 1935.

## II.
## The Original Beginning of the Vaiśeṣika Sūtras
## [E/VII/1-6]

### Preliminary Remarks

When the Centre of South Asian Studies of the School of Oriental and African Studies, University of London, was planning an international symposium on "Aspects of Religion in South Asia" Arnold Kunst also invited Frauwallner. For health reasons Frauwallner could not personally attend, but promised to send an article, the title of which was to be: "Das Eindringen der religiösen Strömungen in die alten philosophischen Systeme, als Beispiel am Vaiśeṣikam gezeigt" (letter to A. Kunst on November 3, 1966: "The Penetration of Religious Streams into the Old Philosophical Systems Shown with Vaiśeṣikam as an Example").

On March 15, 1970 he sent the article entitled "Der ursprüngliche Anfang der Vaiśeṣika-Sūtren" (The Original Beginning of the Vaiśeṣika Sūtras) to London. Afterwards Kunst wrote a summary "The original text of the initial verses in the Vaiśeṣika Sūtras" which he forwarded to the participants together with the article written in German. Finally, the German version of the article was made accessible in a hectographic form in a convolute of the School of Oriental and African Studies: "Seminar on Aspects of Religion in South Asia". Since a publication of all these articles could not be planned (letter from A. Kunst, February 16, 1976), the article is included in the present volume.

The essay was written in the early fifties, in fact in connection with a critical study of the Vaiśeṣika Sūtras, on which he worked at the same time as on the second volume of "Geschichte der indischen Philosophie" (Salzburg, 1956) (cf. ibid., p. 314 note 1; p. 316 n. 1; p. 339, note 387).[1] The notes have been partly supplemented and rearranged.

*

The religious streams which emerged strongly in the early years of the Christian millennium also exerted an influence upon the old philosophical systems. However, this influence was different in the different schools. This is clearly evident in the doctrine of a supreme God. It hardly had any access into the classical Sāṃkhya system which at that time was already paralyzed and declining. And the branch of the school which accepted the notion of a supreme God, did not attain any great importance. By way of example one can compare how Śāntarakṣita

---

[1] This incomplete study is part of his bequest (E/II/1-66). The text of the sūtras has been completed. However, since new literature in the field would have to be included and the critical apparatus completed and supplemented, the work is not suitable for publication in this condition.

dismisses the *seśvaraṃ sāṃkhyam* in his *Tattvasaṃgrahaḥ* when attacking *īśvaravādaḥ*.[2]

It is quite different with Vaiśeṣikam. In it we see clearly how the doctrine of a supreme God gradually forced its way and became established. The sūtras do not as yet recognize the concept of God, nor even Candramati's *Daśapadārthaśāstram*. And in his *Nyāyavārttikam* Uddyotakara still deals with the Vaiśeṣika polemic against *īśvaraḥ*.[3] On the other hand, for Praśastapāda *maheśvaraḥ* is already the creator of the world and in his introductory verse to the *Padārthadharmasaṃgrahaḥ* he professes his belief. That it was still known at that time that this was a later interpolation into the old system, is evident from the polemic in the commentary to the *Sāṃkhyakārikā* called *Yuktidīpikā*, which belongs more or less to the same period.[4] After showing in detail that the author of the *Vaiśeṣika Sūtras* does not recognize *īśvaraḥ*, the author concludes with the words: *evaṃ kāṇādānām īśvaro 'stīti pāśupatopajñam etat*. According to him, then, the doctrine of a supreme God was introduced into the system by Śiva devotees.

The matter is again quite different with the youngest of these systems, the Nyāyaḥ. In it the concept of God appears in the *sūtras* themselves and quickly gains importance. And soon afterwards the doctrine of a supreme God becomes one of the most significant teachings of the school. One of the most famous works of the old Nyāyaḥ, Udayana's *Nyāyakusumāñjaliḥ* serves as a proof for the existence of God. Even in Navyanyāyaḥ, a separate section in Gaṅgeśa's *Tattvacintāmaṇiḥ* is dedicated to this subject.

However, the influence of the religious trends upon the philosophical systems is evident not only in the doctrine of God. It is perceivable elsewhere as well. In the orthodox tradition the first few statements of the Vaiśeṣika Sūtras are as follows:[5]

*athāto dharmaṃ vyākhyāsyāmaḥ* (1)
*yato 'bhyudayaniḥśreyasasiddhiḥ sa dharmaḥ* (2)

---

[2] TS 94-109.

[3] NV 459, 3-15 and 460, 5-15.

[4] YD[1] 87, 14-88, 5 = YD[2] 72, 22-73, 9.

[5] The fourth sūtram does not appear in the Vaiseṣika Sūtras with Candrānanda's commentary (VSū[1]), nor with the anonymous commentary published by Anantalal Thakur (VSū[2]). However, the reference to the six *padārthāḥ* at the beginning is essential.

*tadvacanād āmnāyasya prāmāṇyam* (3)
*dharmaviśeṣaprasūtād dravyaguṇakarmasāmānyaviśeṣasamavāyānāṃ padārthānāṃ sādharmyavaidharmyābhyāṃ tattvajñānān niḥśreyasam* (4)

In this way the Vaiśeṣika system is characterized as a doctrine of liberation. It is nonetheless clear that this contradicts the spirit of the system, because Vaiśeṣika is pure natural philosophy, which attempts to understand and explain the world of phenomena, and has nothing to do with a doctrine of liberation. And this is not just a European impression. Indians have also felt it. Thus, for example, Durveka says in his *Arcaṭālokaḥ: nāpy ādivākye saty apy āśvāso yujyate, anyapratijñātavatām apy anyavyutpādanadarśanāt, yathā 'athāto dharmaṃ vyākhyāsyāmaḥ' iti pratijñāya ṣaṭpadārthapratipādanaṃ kaṇādasya.*[6] It seems reasonable, however, to suggest that the above quoted beginning of the Vaiśeṣika Sūtras is a later addition which, under the influence of the religious trends, replaced another, older commencement. What, then, was this other beginning?

Fortunately, there are clues making it possible to answer this question with some probability. In Vyomaśiva's *Vyomavatī* we twice find the same sentence with a slight difference in the following manner: *'yad iha bhāvarūpaṃ tat sarvaṃ mayopasaṃkhyātavyam' iti pratijñā muneḥ* and *pratijñātaṃ ca maharṣiṇā 'yad bhāvarūpaṃ tat sarvam abhidhāsyāmi' iti.*[7] Udayana quotes the same sentence in his *Kiraṇāvalī* in the following way: *atra hetuḥ 'pṛthag anabhidhānāt' sarvārthopadeśapravṛttena maharṣiṇā pratijñātaṃ hi tena 'yad bhāvarūpaṃ tat sarvam abhidhāsyāmaḥ' iti.*[8] This sentence sounds like the start of a *sūtram* and is explicitly ascribed to Kaṇāda. If we consider, further, that in Lokāyatam - whose association with Vaiśeṣikam was pointed out quite early[9] - the beginning of the *sūtras* were: *athātas tattvaṃ vyākhyāsyāmaḥ,*[10] then it is possible to regard the said sentence as the original beginning of the Vaiśeṣika Sūtras which - even after its replacement

---

6 HBTĀ 241, 22-24.

7 Vyom 47, 13f., and 492, 24f.

8 Kir[1] 227, 10-13 = Kir[2] 482, 14-483, 1.

9 Eg., H. Jacobi: *Die Entwicklung der Gottesidee bei den Indern,* Bonn und Leipzig, 1923, 43.

10 NM[1] 64, 6 = NM[2] 59, 28.

by the later revision,[11] be it through a direct or indirect tradition - continued to be known up until Udayana's time.

If this was the beginning then how are we to imagine the sequel in the old Vaiśeşika Sūtras? There are clues even to this question. In his *Nyāyapraveśakavṛttiḥ* the Jaina polyhistor Haribhadra describes the basic features of the Vaiśeşika theory of categories in the following way:[12]

*tasya siddhānto dravyaguṇakarmasāmānyaviśeṣasamavāyaḥ ṣaṭ padārthāḥ. tataḥ pṛthivy āpas tejo vāyur ākāśaṃ kālo dig ātmā mana iti dravyāṇi. guṇāś caturviṃśatiḥ. rūparasagandhasparśasaṃkhyā-parimāṇāni pṛthaktvaṃ saṃyogavibhāgau paratvāparatve buddhiḥ sukhaduḥkhecchādveṣāḥ prayatnaś ceti sūtroktāḥ. caśabdād dravya-tvaṃ gurutvaṃ saṃskāraḥ sneho dharmādharmau śabdaś ceti. evaṃ caturviṃśatir guṇāḥ. pañca karmāṇi, tad yathā utkṣepaṇam avakṣepa-ṇam ākuñcanaṃ prasāraṇaṃ gamanam iti karmāṇi. gamanagraha-ṇād brahmaṇarecaṇaspandanādyavarodhaḥ. sāmānyaṃ dvividhaṃ param aparaṃ ceti. tatra paraṃ sattā bhāvo mahāsāmānyam iti coc-yate. aparaṃ dravyatvādi.*

A glance at this shows that Haribhadra, at least at the beginning, follows the wording of the Vaiśeşika Sūtras. *pṛthivy āpas tejo vāyur ākāśaṃ kālo dig ātmā mana iti dravyāṇi* and *utkṣepaṇam avakṣepa-ṇam ākuñcanaṃ prasāraṇaṃ gamanam iti karmāṇi* literally corres-pond to sūtras I, 1, 5 and I, 1, 7. *rūparasagandhasparśasaṃkhyāpari-māṇāni pṛthaktvaṃ saṃyogavibhāgau paratvāparatve buddhiḥ sukha-duḥkhecchādveṣāḥ prayatnaś ceti* is hardly different from I, 1, 6. Under these circumstances it seems to me that we can also regard the words *dravyaguṇakarmasāmānyaviśeṣasamavāyāḥ ṣaṭ padārthāḥ* as a sūtram. An account of the theory of categories requires, at the outset, naming and enumerating the categories, and this is given here in the shortest, sūtra-like form.

If we link these with the sūtram established above as the first, then we have the original beginning of the Vaiśeşika Sūtras as follows:

*yad (iha) bhāvarūpaṃ tat sarvam abhidhāsyāmaḥ* (1)
*dravyaguṇakarmasāmānyaviśeṣasamavāyāḥ ṣaṭ padārthāḥ* (2)

---

[11] Vyomaśiva had already known the new beginning, see Vyom 20, 28f.

[12] NPV 28, 25ff.

*pṛthivy āpas tejo vāyur ākāśaṃ kālo dig ātmā mana iti dravyāṇi* (3) etc.

There is no mention of any doctrine of liberation here, but the presentation of the topic, the natural philosophy of the system, begins in a sober and factual way.

The following also speaks in favour of our starting point. In the Nyāya Sūtras the ninth sūtram of the first āhnikam of the first adhyāyaḥ runs as follows:

*ātmaśarīrendriyārthabuddhimanaḥpravṛttidoṣapretyabhāvaphaladuḥkhāpavargās tu prameyam* (9)

Here *prameyam* is enumerated, i.e., the objects whose knowledge is to be conveyed, and these are the very objects whose knowledge is important for liberation. These objects are explained one after the other by Pakṣilasvāmin in his *Nyāyabhāṣyam*. He then concludes with the remark: *asty anyad api dravyaguṇakarmasāmānyaviśeṣasamavāyāḥ prameyam, tadbhedena cāparisaṃkhyeyam. asya tu tattvajñānād apavargo mithyājñānāt saṃsāra ity ata etad upadiṣṭaṃ viśeṣeṇeti.*[13] Thus, there also are other objects whose knowledge could be conveyed, namely, the categories of Vaiśeṣikam. However, through the knowledge of what is at hand, i.e., what is mentioned in the sūtram, liberation can be achieved, and that is why they [the categories] are taught here. Thus, it is clearly and plainly expressed that, for Pakṣilasvāmin, Vaiśeṣikam was not a doctrine of liberation. And the words *dravyaguṇakarmasāmānyaviśeṣasamavāyāḥ prameyam* apparently refer to what we have established as the second sūtram.[14] He therefore still had the old beginning of the Vaiśeṣika Sūtras in mind, which had not yet been presented as a doctrine of liberation.

Now for the last question. How did the transformation of the beginning of the Vaiśeṣika Sutras take place? Praśastapāda begins his *Padārthadharmasaṃgrahaḥ* with the words: *dravyaguṇakarmasāmānyaviśeṣasamavāyānāṃ ṣaṇṇāṃ padārthānāṃ sādharmyavaidharmyatattvajñānaṃ niḥśreyasahetuḥ. tac ceśvaracodanābhivyaktād dharmād eva.* It has always been noticed that these words echo the beginning of the sūtras but it was seen as Praśastapāda's dependence on the sūtras.

---

[13] NBh 88, 16-19.

[14] Pakṣilasvāmin had to say *prameyam* because of its contrast to the quoted Nyāya Sūtram.

Now we would rather judge the relation the other way round. Just as Praśastapāda introduced *īśvaraḥ* into the system, so too did he hallmark it as a doctrine of liberation. And when, in the subsequent centuries, his work had become the standard presentation of the Vaiśeṣika system, the beginning of the sūtras was adapted in line with his work. This new beginning soon received general recognition. Vyomaśiva already knows it. Soon afterwards there also seem to have been standard commentaries written to this form of the sūtras. In Sucaritamiśra's *Kāśikā* we read: '*śiṣyapraśnāntaraṃ kaṇabhujā tantraṃ praṇītam' ity arthamālāyām uktam*. Further: *yathā 'athāto dharmaṃ vyākhyāsyāmaḥ' iti śiṣyapraśnānantaraṃ śāstraṃ praṇayāma iti kāśyapenoktam iti*. And: *kāṇāde hi tantre kriyānantaryarūpaḥ sambandho darśitaḥ. evaṃ hi tatra bhāṣyakāreṇoktaṃ 'ko dharma ityādikān śiṣyenodīritān pañca praśnān apekṣyāha athāto dharmaṃ vyākhyāsyāmaḥ' iti*.[15] So, at least in the ninth century there had already been a detailed bhāṣyam to the sūtras in their new form.

In summarizing our results we can say: Vaiśeṣikam was originally pure natural philosophy and the beginning of the sūtras was correspondingly composed. Under the influence of the religious trends which were gaining in strength, the doctrine of a supreme God was introduced into the system in the middle of the first millennium of the Christian era and adopted by Praśastapāda. Further, it was Praśastapāda who explained the system as a doctrine of liberation. When his work became established as the standard presentation of Vaiśeṣikam, this conception generally pervaded. And, finally, even the beginning of the sūtras was replaced by a new one which introduced the system as a doctrine of liberation.

---

[15] ŚVṬ 7, 25; further, 8, 20f. and 8, 26ff.

**Literature**


Kir *Kiraṇāvalī* (Udayana): 1. Ed. Vindhyeśvarī Prasāda Dvivedī. (BSS 9) Benares 1919; 2. Ed. Śiva Chandra Sarvabhauma, Narendra Chandra Vedantatirtha. (BI 200) Calcutta 1911-1912, 1956.

NBh *Nyāyabhāṣyam* (Pakṣilasvāmin): Ed. Lakṣmaṇa Śāstrī and Śrīrāma Śāstrī (KSS 43) Benares 1920.

NM *Nyāyamañjarī* (Jayantabhaṭṭa): 1. Ed. Gaṅgādhara Śāstrī Tailaṅga. (VizSS 8) Benares 1895; 2. Ed. S.N. Śukla (KSS 106) Benares 1936.

NPV *Nyāyapraveśavṛttiḥ* (Haribhadra): *The Nyāyapraveśa Part I. Sanskrit Text with Commentaries.* Ed. A.B. Dhruva. (GOS 38) Baroda 1930.

NV *Nyāyavārttikam* (Uddyotakara): Ed. V. Prasad Dwivedi, Lakshmana Sastri. (KSS 33) Benares 1916.

HBTĀ *Hetubinduṭīkālokaḥ* (Durvekamiśra): *Hetubinduṭīkā of Bhaṭṭa Arcaṭa with the Sub-Commentary entitled Āloka of Durveka Miśra.* Ed. S. Sanghavi and Muni Jinavijayaji. (GOS 113) Baroda 1949.

ŚVṬ *Ślokavārttikaṭīkā, Kāśikā* (Sucaritamiśra): Ed. Sāmbaśiva Śāstrī. (TrivSS 90, 99, 150) Trivandrum 1926 ff.

TS *Tattvasaṅgrahaḥ* (Śāntarakṣita): Ed. E. Krishnamacharya. 2 vols. (GOS 30, 31) Baroda 1926.

Vyom *Vyomavatī* (Vyomaśiva): *The Praśastapādabhāṣyam by Praśasta Devāchārya with Commentaries.* Ed. G. Kavirāj. (ChSS 61) Benares 1930

VSū *Vaiśeṣikasūtram:* 1. *Vaiśeṣikasūtram of Kaṇāda with the Commentary of Candrānanda.* Ed. Muni Jambuvijayaji. (GOS 136) Baroda 1961; 2. *Vaiśeṣikadarśana of Kaṇāda with an Anonymous Commentary.* Ed. A. Thakur. [MIS 5) Darbhanga 1957.

YD *Yuktidīpikā*: 1. Ed. P. Chakravarti. (CSS 23) Calcutta 1938; 2. Ed. R. Ch. Pandeya. Delhi 1967.

# III.

## Navyanyāyaḥ
## [K/XV/15, 1-14]

### Preliminary Remarks

Frauwallner worked on the Navyanyāya School from Summer 1962[1] until 1967. At the end of this period the following two summaries were written as articles intended for philosophico-historical surveys.

The first, longer article was planned for the new edition of "Ueberwegs Grundriß der Geschichte der Philosophie" (Ueberweg's Outline of the History of Philosophy). At the beginning Frauwallner was only a collaborator for Vol. VII: The Philosophy of India and East-Asia but, however, after his suggestions for the division of this volume,[2] he was entrusted with the editorship of the first half of the volume "Die Philosophie Indiens" (The Philosophy of India)[3]. After the death of Paul Wilpert, the general editor, (January 1, 1967) Frauwallner resigned from this task.[4]

The present article was planned as a draft for the Indian volume,[5] which was to be printed and submitted to the collaborators, replacing the plan circulated by the publishers. He began detailed work on the draft at the end of 1966, which was "interrupted for the time being"[6], because of Wilpert's death. This interruption was to remain. The article is, therefore, not quite complete. Two large gaps are evident: first, it lacks a description of the tradition of the Mahāvidyā logic[7] and, second, a description of the "Hochblüte der Kommentatoren" (Golden Age of the Commentators) of Gaṅgeśa's work.[8] Also, the structure of the article has not been fully carried through.

The second article was intended for the "Lexikon der Philosophie", (Encyclopaedia of Philosophy) a revision of the Enciclopedia Filosofica, planned, among others, by Walter Brugger in 1965. Frauwallner agreed to write an article for it entitled "Navya-Nyāyaḥ"[9] and he sent it on December 15, 1969.[10] However, the

---

1 Letter to G. Bhattacharya on April 10, 1963 [Ko/III/24].

2 Letter to Schwabe & Co., Basel, January 16, 1966 [Ko/V/279].

3 Letter from Schwabe & Co., Basel, May 4, 1966 [Ko/V/297].

4 Letter to Schwabe & Co., Basel, March 2, 1967 [Ko/V/313].

5 Notes to the meeting in Basel, March 23, 1966 [Ko/V/286r].

6 Letter to Schwabe & Co., Basel, March 2, 1967 [Ko/V/313].

7 In the Ms it is temporarily bracketed with the remark "to be completed" [K/XV/6]. There are no such notes in the bequest.

8 A section in the present article corresponds to it [c/f. p. 60 = K/XV/7].

9 Letter to the editors, April 9, 1969 [Ko/V/199].

10 A note on the letter from the editors, May 8, 1969 [Ko/V/200].

work on the Encyclopaedia in the planned form was abandoned in 1971 and I am not aware of an intended publication in a reduced form.

*

The position in the field of Navyanyāyaḥ is especially inconvenient. Very little of the vast literature, of which a large part is extant, has been published. Even the works of the outstanding representatives of the school are hardly accessible. What is often published are primitive handbooks and texts for the school. There is also a lack of academic presentations and investigations. A more detailed treatment in books and treatises which report about the authors and their works, has revealed only a superficial history of the system. There are no works on the system itself. What is available till now are but poor sketches based on the contemporary activities of schools. European research has dealt almost exclusively with the primitive handbooks.

Under these circumstances an account of the entire system was impossible. It is therefore attempted here at least to give a short characterization based on a specific area and to draw the basic lines of development. For this purpose I have chosen the theory of inference, which is central to the system, and within this, the most dealt with and controversial problem of the theory of pervasion. This sketch is based on the main works of the school. The usual handbooks are not dealt with, but referred to only in passing.

As for the general history of the school, I have made just a selection. It would be meaningless to refer to dozens of authors and works which, at the outset, are empty names for us. I have selected what appeared to be significant and what was necessary to give a clear sequence of the development. The chronology is just an attempt. The accounts of Indian scholars on whom we have to rely nowadays, are often contradictory and based, to a large degree, on local tradition which can only be verified on location. It is therefore attempted to present a chronology which may serve at least as a relative chronology, on the basis of the few clues which appear to be reliable.

At about the middle of the twelfth century a new development was introduced in Nyāyaḥ, which was referred to as the new school of logic, Navyanyāyaḥ. It contains a new way of considering the relations on which inference is based and, thereby, created a wealth of new terms and problems. Navyanyāyaḥ may be divided broadly into the following periods:

1. The period of its origin, in which the new way of examination was established and organized. It reaches its conclusion in the great, condensed work of Gaṅgeśa. The further development of the school has its impact, above all, in the commentaries to this work. Accordingly one has to distinguish:

2. The period of the old commentators. Here the new terms were analyzed and elaborated. It reaches its climax in about the second half of the fifteenth century and its last representative is Raghunātha Śiromaṇi. Until then the centre of the school was in Mithilā. With Raghunātha the leadership is transferred to Bengal.

3. The period of the later commentators who comment especially upon Raghunātha's works, in which they completed in all directions the system adopted by him. This period ended towards the end of the seventeenth century.

4. The late period, which goes on into contemporary times. Here the system becomes paralyzed. There are no more outstanding representatives in this period.

Alongside this new school, the old Nyāyaḥ recedes completely into the background. Its representatives are largely forgotten. Only Udayana continued to be regarded as "the master" (ācāryaḥ) and his works were repeatedly commented upon. Otherwise, the old sūtras were commented on only occasionally, in accordance with the dependence on tradition of the time and its respect for the sacred tradition.

By this time Vaiśeṣikam had entirely lost its significance as an independent system. It was promoted and further developed only through the representatives of Navyanyāyaḥ, especially in Udayana's and Śrīvallabha's commentaries to the Vaiśeṣika works. For the rest, here too occasionally, in accordance with the dependence on tradition, commentaries on the Sūtras or Praśastapāda's *Padārthadharmasaṃgrahaḥ* were written.

Finally, the handbooks need to be mentioned which, because of their popularity and wide circulation, were continuously written. Despite their poor content the research until now has unfortunately dealt more with them than with the basic works of the school.

*

On the basis of what we know today, we cannot say who first gave the impulse for the emergence of Navyanyāyaḥ. Śivāditya Miśra may have belonged to the period of the beginning of the system. A long list of names from the time before Gaṅgeśa has come down to us as, for example, Divākara, Prabhākara Upādhyāya, Sondaḍa (or Sondala), Taraṇi Miśra, Śaśadhara and Maṇikaṇṭha. For the present, most of them, however, are mere names. Only works by Śaśadhara and Maṇikaṇṭha are extant and published. This first period is concluded by Gaṅgeśa who condensed everything achieved until then in a major work, on which the subsequent development is built. Apart from Gaṅgeśa is his son Vardhamāna who supplements his father's work with numerous commentaries, especially on Udayana's writings.

In this period, in addition to numerous independent texts, commentaries to Udayana's Nyāya works were also written, for example, by Divākara, Prabhākara and, as pointed out, by Vardhamāna. Further, Rāghava, a student of Vādīndra, wrote a commentary to Bhāsarvajña's *Nyāyasāraḥ*.

As for Vaiśeṣika works during this period, there is a commentary to the Sūtras by Vādīndra, and a short, anonymous commentary that follows Vādīndra. Furthermore, Udayana's *Kiraṇāvalī* was repeatedly commented on, e.g., by Vādīndra, Divākara, Prabhākara and Vardhamāna. The same with Śrīvallabha's *Nyāyalīlāvatī* by Prabhākara and Vardhamāna.

The episode of the Mahāvidyā syllogisms also belongs to the beginning of this period. Towards the end of the twelfth century Paṇḍit Kulārka, about whom nothing further is known, drew up a row of bold fallacies which, though intended ultimately to serve the purpose of proving the transitoriness of sound according to Nyāya-Vaiśeṣikam, could also be used in general. They first caused a stir. Śivāditya dealt with them, then they were criticized in detail by Vādīndra and, gradually, they were forgotten. Maṇikaṇṭha had still dealt with them. Gaṅgeśa, however, did not consider them anymore.

**Extant Works, Editions**

**Śivāditya.** *Saptapadārthī*, with the com. Mitabhāṣiṇī by Mādhava Sarasvatī, ed. by Rāmaśāstrī Tailanga, Benares 1893 (VizSS 8); with the com. Padārthacandrikā by Śeṣānanta, ed. with introduction and notes by V.S. Ghāte, Bombay 1909; with Mādhava's Mitabhāṣiṇī, Śeṣānanta's Padārthacandrikā and Balabhadra's Sandarbha, critically edited from Original Manuscripts, with Extracts from Jinavardhana's Commentary, Introduction, Notes, Various Readings and Indices, by Amarendra Mohan Bhattacharya and Narendra Chandra Bagchi Bhattacharya, Calcutta 1934 (CSS 8).

**Śaśadhara.** *Nyāyasiddhāntadīpaḥ*, with the com. Nyāyasiddhāntadīpaprabhā by Śeṣānanta, ed. by Vindhyeśvarī Prasād Dvivedī, Benares 1924, (Pandit Reprint).

**Maṇikaṇṭha.** *Nyāyaratnam*, with the com. Dyutimālikā by Nṛsiṃhayajvan, critically ed. with Introduction by V. Subrahmanya Śāstrī and V. Krishnamacharya, Madras 1953 (MGOS 104).

**Gaṅgeśa.** *Tattvacintāmaṇiḥ*, with the com. Tattvacintāmaṇirahasyam by Mathurānātha Tarkavāgīśa, ed. by Kāmākhyānātha Tarkavāgīśa, 4 vols., Calcutta 1884-1901 (BI 98) (the only complete edition; it contains, especially where Mathurānātha's commentary is lacking, also sections of other commentaries); with the com. Ālokaḥ by Jayadeva Miśra, Ālokadarpanaḥ by Maheśa Ṭhakkura, Ālokakaṇṭakoddhāraḥ by Madhusūdana Ṭhakkura and Pragalbhī by Pragalbha, ed. by Sūryanārāyaṇa Śarma Śukla, Benares 1939 (PWSBhT 78/1; upto the end of the Maṅgalavādaḥ in the Pratyakṣakhaṇḍaḥ); with the com. Ālokaḥ by Pakṣadhara Miśra and Darpanaḥ by Maheśa Ṭhakkura, ed. by Umesha Mishra and Śaśinātha Śarma Jhā, Darbhanga 1957 (MVG 1/1; upto the end of the Prāmāṇyavādaḥ in the Pratyakṣakhaṇḍaḥ). Parts of the basic text are also included in the different editions of the commentaries.

**Vardhamāna.** *Pariśiṣṭaprakāśaḥ* in the edition of the *Nyāyapariśiṣṭam* (CSS 22); *Nyāyanibhandaprakāśaḥ* in the edition of the *Nyāyavārttikatātparyapariśuddhiḥ* (BI 205); *Kiraṇāvalīprakāśaḥ* in the edition of the *Kiraṇāvalī* (BI 200); *Kusumāñjaliprakāśaḥ* in the edition of the *Kusumāñjaliḥ* (KSS 30); *Līlāvatīprakāśaḥ* in the edition of the Nyāyalīlāvatī (ChSS 64).

**Vādīndra.** *Mahāvidyāviḍambanam* with Ānandapūrṇa's com. (only of the first section) and the Vyākhyānadīpikā by Bhuvanasundara Sūri, and, further, the Laghumahāvidyāviḍambanam by Buvanasundara Sūri, the Daśaślokīmahāvidyāsūtram by Kulārka Paṇḍita and an anonymous Mahāvidyāvivaraṇam with Bhuvanasundara Sūri's com., ed. with Introduction and Appendices by Mangesh Ramakrishna Telang, Baroda 1920 (GOS 12); *Dravyakiraṇāvalīṭīkā*, as an appendix to the edition of the *Kiraṇāvalī* (BI 200); *Rasasāraḥ*, ed. by Gopīnātha Kavirāja, Benares 1922 (PWSBhT 5).

**The anonymous commentary to the Vaiśeṣika Sūtras** was published under the title *Vaiśeṣikadarśana of Kaṇāda, with an anonymous commentary*, ed. by Anantalal Thakur, Darbhanga 1957 (MVG 5).

*

The new view which forms the basis of Navyanyāyaḥ is the attempt to form a clear picture of the relations lying at the basis of inference in the framework of Vaiśeṣika thought, and to strive to linguistically formulate it. The old view adopted from Buddhist logic continued to be valid, viz., that in an inference the question was one of a relation between two properties (*dharmaḥ*) of a property-bearer (*dharmī*). But a separate expression (*adhikaraṇam*) was used for the bearer and one spoke of the bearer of the probandum (*sādhyādhikaraṇam*) and of the bearer of the probans (*sādhanādhikaraṇam*). When the old Nyāyaḥ spoke of the occurrence in instances of the same kind (*sapakṣe sattvam*), this now meant the occurence in the bearer of the probandum (*sādhyavadvṛttitvam*) or its having a common bearer with the probandum (*sādhyasāmānādhikaraṇyam*), etc. In this context absence (*abhāvaḥ*) plays a significant role. Nyāyaḥ had already known the term absence for a long time, which was interpreted as something real, in keeping with the realism of the school. Accordingly, the absence of a thing was not simply its lack, but it was, rather, the presence of its absence. Four kinds of absence were thus distinguished: prior absence (*prāgabhāvaḥ*), absence through decay (*pradhvaṃsābhāvaḥ*), complete absence (*atyantābhavaḥ*), and mutual absence (*anyonyābhāvaḥ*).

Moreover, each absence on its own has no definite character. This is rather based on the counterpositive (*pratiyogī*) to which it is in relation.

With the help of these and similar terms the adopted definitions were transformed. The definition of pervasion [or concomitance] (*vyāptiḥ*) is a good example. The various earlier definitions which were sought to be transformed in this way, were not satisfactory. In order to understand the definition which was basic to the later development, it would be convenient to begin with the two old conditions, occurrence in instances of the same kind (*sapakṣe sattvam*) and absence in a counter instance (*vipakṣe asattvam*). In the terminology of Navya-nyāyaḥ existence in instances of the same kind meant, as already stated, the occurrence of the bearer of the probandum (*sādhyavadvṛttitvam* or *sādhyasāmānādhikaraṇyam*). Its lack in a counter instance, accordingly, then had to mean its absence in the bearer of the absence of the probandum (*sādhyābhāvavadavṛttitvam*). Both conditions would have had to be connected in one definition. It was argued against this that such a definition does not satisfy the case of a reason that is exclusively positive (*kevalānvayī hetuḥ*), because here there is no absence of the probandum. So the aim was to find a formulation which avoided this expression. The absence of the probandum was defined by the probandum as its counterpositive (*pratiyogī*). Therefore, instead of saying that the cause must not occur in the bearer of the absence of the probandum, it was stated that it should occur only in the bearer of an absence, whose counterpositive is not the probandum. And when this was combined with the first condition, its occurrence in the bearer of the probandum, the following definition was arrived at: "Pervasion obtains when the probans occurs in the same bearer as the probandum, which is not the counterpositive of a complete absence which occurs together with the probans in the same bearer" (*sādhanavanniṣṭhātyantābhāvāpratiyogisādhyasāmānādhikaraṇyam*). This definition served as the basis for the further development and was constantly supplemented and improved. Already with Gaṅgeśa we find it in the following expanded form: "Pervasion means that it (the reason) has the same bearer as what is not limited by the limitor of the counterpositiveness of a complete absence which has the same bearer (as the reason), but does not have the same bearer as (its own) counterpositive" (*pratiyogyasāmānādhikaraṇayatsāmānādhikaraṇātyantābhāvapratiyogitāvacchedakāvachinnaṃ yan na bhavati, tena samaṃ tasya sāmānādhikaraṇyaṃ vyāptiḥ*). (See the next section for the significance of the additions). All the formulations of the old Nyāyaḥ were transformed accordingly. But this example may suffice.

Together with the development of Navyanyāyaḥ there was a reorganization of the Vaiśeṣika system. The relations, to which the terms of the Vaiśeṣika system were now applied, were in fact far removed from the original conception of the system. It therefore required adaptation and supplementation. And these followed in the commentaries which were written to Udayana's and Śrīvallabha's Vaiśeṣika works.

A separate episode, apart from the mainstream of the development, is represented by the Mahāvidyā conclusions.[11]

Śivāditya Miśra (c.1200 AD) has until now been known only through a handbook on Vaiśeṣika, the *Saptapadārthī*, which hardly reveals his true significance. That he includes absence (*abhāvaḥ*) as a seventh category, in addition to the traditional six, has only a formal significance, since the theory of absence was dealt with by the school long before him. The work *Lakṣaṇamālā* is known only through quotations.[12] An extant though unpublished smaller work on logic is the *Hetukhaṇḍanam*. Quotations from an *Upādhivārttikam* and an *Arthāpattivārttikam* indicate extensive commentary writing. Under the present circumstances it is not possible to give an appreciation of his achievement, and has to be left to later research.

Two commentaries by Divākara Upādhyāya (first half of the thirteenth century) on Udayana's works are at least in parts extant, though not published: a *Nyāyanibandhoddyotaḥ* on the *Tātparyapariśuddhiḥ*, and a commentary to the *Kusumāñjaliḥ* called *Parimalaḥ*. There are also references to commentaries on the *Ātmatattvavivekaḥ*, on the *Kiraṇāvalī*, as well as on Śrīharṣa's *Khaṇḍanakhaṇḍakhādyam*. Prabhākara Upādhyāya (middle of the thirteenth century) is known at present only through quotations, about whom also commentaries to Udayana's *Tātparyapariśuddhiḥ*, *Kusumāñjaliḥ* and *Kiraṇāvalī*, and to Śrīvallabha's *Nyāyalīlāvatī* are mentioned.

To the list of most important precursors to Gaṅgeśa, we have to add Sondaḍa Upādhyāya and Taraṇi Miśra (second half of the 13th

---

[11] [The presentation of these conclusions is missing].

[12] The work published under this name is actually by Udayana (see Udayana).

century), even though we know them only through quotations. Sondaḍa is especially mentioned as a representative of the theory of *vyadhikaraṇadharmāvacchinnapratiyogikābhāvaḥ* (see next section). Taraṇi is often cited as the author of a *Ratnakośaḥ*.

Works by Śaśadhara Ācārya (second half of the thirteenth century) and Maṇikaṇṭha Miśra (c.1300 AD) are extant. Śaśadhara's *Nyāyasiddhāntadīpaḥ*, in 26 loosely arranged sections, deals not only with logical questions, but also with controversial terms of Vaiśeṣika, with the philosophy of language, with liberation, etc. With him the theories evince a well advanced degree of development. That his influence on Gaṅgeśa was relatively small may be due less to the difference in time, as to the affiliation to another school. So, as the immediate forerunner to Gaṅgeśa, we may instead regard Maṇikaṇṭha, from whose works Gaṅgeśa directly draws a great deal. His work, the *Nyāyaratnam*, also consists of loosely connected sections limited though to logic and the dialectical categories of Nyāyaḥ, in which it largely follows the sequence of the Nyāya Sūtras.

In marked contrast to these loosely developed works stands the grand creation by Gaṅgeśa (c.1290-1350 AD), the *Tattvacintāmaṇiḥ*. What he himself achieved for the subsequent development of the doctrine cannot be judged for certain in the present state of our knowledge. In any case, his achievement as a systematizer was important. He strictly limited himself to epistemology, the actual core of the system. His work is thus divided into four books, according to the four means of cognition (*pramāṇam*) of Nyāyaḥ: perception, inference, comparison, and verbal testimony. Within this narrow framework, however, he combined all the relevant material in a clear structure, with an hitherto unknown completeness. The old theories which could be regarded as having been surpassed are summarized in a long pūrvapakṣaḥ. Then follows his own approved teaching as siddhāntaḥ. Other theories of the previous period which appeared to him to deserve attention, are added to the siddhāntaḥ. Even though in a few details the presentation of the material may not always appear satisfactory, nonetheless, on the whole his achievement was outstanding and the consequences immense. Everything significant that was later achieved, closely followed his work, i.e., in the customary Indian way of writing commentaries and sub-commentaries. After Gaṅgeśa Nyāyaḥ can hardly be considered a self-contained philosophical system: it is and remained essentially epistemology. Vaiśeṣika now definitively became an auxiliary to Nyāyaḥ.

Since Gaṅgeśa was so preoccupied with his great work, he found no time for the traditional composition of commentaries to the existing classics of the system. This void was filled by his son Vardhamāna Upādhyāya (c.1315-1375 AD). He wrote commentaries to all the major works of Udayana, calling them all *prakāśaḥ*: a *Nyāyanibandhaprakāśaḥ* to the *Tātparyapariśuddhiḥ*, a *Nyāyapariśiṣṭaprakāśaḥ* to the *Prabodhasiddhiḥ*, a *Kusumāñjaliprakāśaḥ*, a *Kiraṇāvalīprakāśaḥ*, the *Bauddhadhikkāraprakāśaḥ*, and, further, a *Līlāvatīprakāśaḥ* to Śrīvallabha's *Nyāyalīlāvatī* and a *Khaṇḍaṇaprakāśaḥ* to Śrīharṣa's *Khaṇḍanakhaṇḍakhādyam*. A commentary to parts of the Nyāya Sūtras is called *Tattvabodhaḥ*. Vardhamāna follows his father substantially in all essential points, even though it does not lack minor deviations.

Bhaṭṭa Vādīndra (first half of the thirteenth century) stands apart from the mainstream development. He was the student of a certain Yogīśvara and was the Dharmādhyakṣaḥ of a King Śrīsiṃha, who may well be identical with King Siṅghana of the Yādava Dynasty (1210-1247 AD). The following works of his are extant: the *Mahāvidyāviḍambanam*, a detailed refutation of the Mahāvidyā syllogisms; further, a commentary to Udayana's *Kiraṇāvalī* in two parts, a *Dravyakiraṇāvalīṭīkā* and the *Rasasāraḥ* to the *Guṇakiraṇāvalī;* and, finally, the *Kaṇādasūtranibandhaḥ* to the Vaiśeṣika Sūtras. Only one work is extant by one of Vādīndra's students, Bhaṭṭa Rāghava, as yet unpublished, the *Nyāyasāravicāraḥ*,[13] a commentary to Bhāsarvajña's *Nyāyasāraḥ*, which was written in 1252 AD.[14]

We may regard Raghunātha Śiromaṇi as the founder of the new direction. The distinctive uniqueness of his work speaks in favour of it. The question about the essence of the basic terms, which occupied a major place with his predecessors, completely recedes into the background in his work. When he does, however, enter into such a discussion he is superficial and glosses over the problems with his trivial formulations. In general, he works with the traditional terms. The most important thing for him is their application. He tests the applicability of the given definitions in the most remote and difficult cases and supplements and transforms them according to need. And, in the process, he develops an astounding phantasy and skilfulness. He especially enjoys

---

[13] [Ed. by Umā Ramaṇa Jhā, Jammu 1976].

[14] [The section before Raghunātha Śiromaṇi, which was to deal with the great commentaries, is missing (c/f. the next article p. 60)].

grappling with intricacies, ensuing from some traditional terms and theses, e.g., that a fact equipped with a determination is not different from the simple one (*viśiṣṭasya anatiriktatā*), that complex properties (*guravo dharmāḥ*) are not valid if they have the same realm as the simple ones, that the lack of two-ness (*dvitvam*) is given when one of the two parts is lacking, and that the remainder can represent the absence of both together (*ubhayābhāvaḥ*). What is more important, though, is that he applies factors which were hardly, if at all, taken into consideration; and this is then continued further by his school. To this belongs especially the connection (*sambandhaḥ*) of the members of an inference with their bearer, in which he also incorporates kinds of connections which were till then not taken into consideration. Further, taking into account the time factor, etc., proved to be important. He strove to consider all these in forming the definitions and, where possible, to work them in.

As an example we may take the definition of pervasion again. Raghunātha's starting point was an expanded form of Gaṅgeśa's definition which runs thus: "When (a reason) has the same bearer as what is delimited by a property, which property does not delimit the counterpositiveness of a constant absence which shares the same bearer as the (reason) which is determined by the outward form, but does not share the same bearer as its own counterpositive, then there is in it a pervasion of a specific (reason) determined by this outward form which is characterized by everything which is delimited by that property" (*pratiyogyasāmānādhikaraṇayadrūpaviśiṣṭasāmānādhikaraṇātyantābhāvapratiyogitānavacchedako yo dharmas, taddharmāvacchinnena kenāpi samaṃ sāmānādhikaraṇyaṃ tadrūpaviśiṣṭasya taddharmāvacchinnayāvannirūpitā vyāptiḥ)*. This definition hardly differs from that of Rucidatta; except that pervasion itself has a more accurate definition which, in turn, is based on a more exact grasp of the term possessing-the-same-bearer (*sāmānādhikaraṇyam*). For, this is an occurrence (*vṛttitvam*) and is as such, considered consistently and realistically, a property which is associated with the bearer in question which, again, is more precisely determined by this very bearer, on the one hand, and by the property, on the other hand, which shares this bearer and which is characteristic (*nirūpakaḥ*) for it [the property].

Raghunātha then proceeds further so that, by making the individual determinations more precise, he adjusts the definition to suit difficult special cases. Finally, the inclusion of connection (*sambandhaḥ*) leads to a remodelling [of the definition]. Three cases come under consideration: the connection of the reason with its bearer; the connection of the result; and, finally, the connection of the counterpositive of the absence occurring in the bearer of the reason. In case this absence, which is to be excluded, is an absence of the result, then the connection of the counterpositive coincides with that of the result and the distinction can be omitted. Raghunātha now incorporates the reference to these connections into the definition of pervasion. Further, for the expression bearer (*adhikaraṇam*) he substitutes participator in the relation (*sambandhī*), through which it becomes possible for him to combine both forms of the definition into a single formulation, i.e., the one that is based on total absence (*atyantābhāvaḥ*) and the one based on mutual absence (*anyonyābhāvaḥ*). Finally, a few difficulties which still occur, give rise to a remodelling of the definition which then takes on the following form: "Pervasion is the occurrence of the reason because of a certain connection in the same bearer with what is delimitated through a certain property, if, in the generality of the counterpositiveness of absence which is attached to the bearer of the reason which is not the bearer of its counterpositive, the limitedness through this very connection and the limitedness through this very property do not obtain at the same time" (*pratiyogyanadhikaraṇahetumanniṣṭhābhāvapratiyogitāsāmānye yatsambandhāvacchinnatvayaddharmāvacinnatvobhayābhāvas, tena sambandhena taddharmāvacchinnasāmānādhikaraṇyaṃ vyāptiḥ*).

But with that it was not enough. Since Raghunātha lays special stress on the term limitorship (*avacchedakatvam*) he strives to determine it precisely. Immediately after the thesis that a limitor is not wider in extension than the limiting (*anatiriktavṛtti-*), he arrives at the following definition for the limiting of the counterpositiveness of the absence occuring in the bearer of the reason: "An occurrence of not going beyond (what is limiting) obtains when no specific generic-propertyness, defined by itself, is connected with the bearer of an absence whose counterpositiveness is thereby delimited, or when it does not delimit the counterpositiveness of an absence which is attached to the participant in the connection of what is defined by itself" (*tadavacchinnapratiyogitākābhāvavadasambaddhasvaviśiṣṭasāmānyakatvaṃ svaviśiṣṭasambandhiniṣṭhābhāvapratiyogitānavacchedakatatkatvaṃ vā*). He now builds the second variant of this definition into his definition of pervasion which then has the following form: "Pervasion is the occurrence of the probans in the same bearer as what is determined by a specific property, if the being delimited through the non-delimiting of the counterpositiveness of the absence, delimited by a kind of determining, [an absence] which is attached to the participant in the connection with something determined by this very property in the case of the generic property of the counterpositiveness of total absence, delimited by the same connection, which [absence] has the same bearer as the probans, does not obtain" (*viśesaṇatāviśeṣāvachinnayaddharmaviśiṣṭa-sambandhiniṣṭhābhāvapratiyogitānavacchedakāvacchedyatvaṃ tatsam-bandhāvacchinnasādhanasāmānādhikaraṇātyantābhāvapratiyogitā-sāmānye nāsti, sādhane taddharmaviśiṣṭasāmānādhikaraṇyaṃ vyā-ptiḥ*). Finally, in the conclusion of the whole discussion on pervasion he gives a few other variants.

This kind of treatment of the material and the same skilfulness in forming definitions and their application in the most diverse cases is evident everywhere in Raghunātha's writings. The form of his work is, however, unsatisfactory. Not only does he strive for brevity but he takes pleasure in contrived and artificial obscurity. He does not speak clearly but gives hints, so that different interpretations are possible. Often important links in the train of thought are left out and the reader has to guess the omissions. It is also characteristic that he avoids to say openly what his own view is. That is why his work is unusually difficult to read. But this obscurity which pretends to be depth of thought, may have contributed, not in a small way, to the reputation which the work enjoyed subsequently.

Through Raghunātha's activity the Bengal school was given a definite direction, which it maintained till contemporary times. Numerous commentaries continued further what he had begun. The terms and viewpoints with which he had worked were systematically applied to all individual cases and worked through. In this way the system was brought to a kind of completion. There was, however, nothing basically new created. More independence is evident, at the most, in the field of language philosophy which at this time came stronger into the foreground and on which also major independent works were written.

It is not surprising that such an activity gradually led to a kind of paralysis. This actually began at the end of the seventeenth century and the situation was not changed by the work of individual, competent scholars, who with a full command of the material, sought to continue working on the usual lines. What was predominant, and remained so, was that the terms and their application which were handed down, were taught and practised as something given. And this is the form in which the school in Bengal even today continues to exist.

Raghunātha Tārkikaśiromaṇi (c.1480-1540), usually called Śiromaṇi in short, is said to have come from a modest background and to have lost his father early. Whatever else is told about him hardly bears any truth. Only his studentship under Vāsudeva Sārvabhauma seems to be somewhat definite. But this may have come to an end soon, when Vāsudeva left Bengal in order to move to Orissa.

The most important of Raghunātha's works is by far his commentary on Gaṅgeśa's *Tattvacintāmaṇiḥ*, the *Tattvacintāmaṇidīdhitiḥ*, especially to the second part, the section on inference. He does not seem to have commented on the third part, on comparison, at all. The commentary on the fourth part, on verbal testimony, is extant only in fragments. The commentary on the second part is also the one in which Raghunātha's grasp and presentation has its greatest impact, and to which, above all, the rich commentary literature which gives the Bengal school its character, is linked.

Apart from his main work Raghunātha wrote commentaries to Udayana's *Ātmatattvavivekaḥ*, called the *Ātmatattvavivekadīdhitiḥ* or the *Ātmatattvavivekabhāvaprakāśaḥ*, and to Vardhamāna's *Kiraṇāvaliprakāśaḥ* and *Nyāyalīlāvatīprakāśaḥ*, the *Kiraṇāvalīprakāśadīdhitiḥ* and the *Nyāyalīlāvatīprakāśadīdhitiḥ*. Further, there are two minor works on language theory, the *Ākhyātavādaḥ* on the meaning of verbal suffixes, and the *Nañvādaḥ* on the meaning of negation. His *Padārthatattvanirūpaṇam*, also called *Padārthakhaṇḍanam*, is noteworthy. Through its exaggerated realism and through the application to an inappropriate object Navyanyāyaḥ had taken the old Vaiśeṣika system to absurdity. Raghunātha had realized this and he attempted to master the difficulties with a criticism of the traditional categories and with the suggestion of new categories. As he explicitly emphasizes, it is an attempt. He did not succeed and was not in a position to present a basically new conception. But it is important for an evaluation of his work that, although he generally gets absorbed in formalism, he was sensitive to these problems and that he tried to cope with them.

# IV.
# Navyanyāyaḥ, an Article for the "Wörterbuch der Philosophie" (Dictionary of Philosophy) [K/XXIX/1-9]

## 1. Essentials of Navyanyāyaḥ:

During the twelfth century a new direction began to emerge in the Indian philosophical school of Nyāyaḥ, out of which the new school of Nyāyaḥ, the Navyanyāyaḥ, developed, which has remained active till the present times. And this development took place above all on the basis of the doctrine of inference. Nyāyaḥ has always been realistic and very early adopted the Vaiśeṣikam doctrine of categories for the basic structure of its epistemology. Thus, it was always assumed that in an inference real things, in the sense of the doctrine of categories, correspond to the process of cognition. However, these ideas were previously not pursued. Now an attempt was made to form a clear picture of these real things and to strive to express them in linguistic formulations.

A good example of this is the definition of the relation between the cause and the result, [namely,] of pervasion (*vyāptiḥ*). It had always been the view that with cause and result two properties came in question, which were attached with one object. In order to express this the old definitions of cause namely, that it must occur only in a thing of the same kind (*sapakṣaḥ*) and must be absent in a thing of a different kind (*vipakṣaḥ*), was so transformed that it was said that it must occur only in the bearers of the probandum and must be absent in the bearers of the absence of the probandum. Here absence (*abhāvaḥ*), according to the old Nyāya view, was regarded as something real which, however, as absence, cannot be associated with qualities, but characterized only by its counterpositive (*pratiyogī*). But now, one wanted to take a special case into consideration, namely, an inference in which there is nothing of a different kind, i.e., one in which one cannot speak of the absence of the probandum. And so the following formulation was selected: that the cause must occur only in the bearer of an absence whose counterpositive is not the probandum. Summarizing the conditions which were obtained in this way, the following definition of pervasion emerged: "Pervasion obtains when the probans occurs in the same bearer with a probandum which is not the counterpositive of a total absence which occurs with the probans in the same bearer". This definition was further elaborated and reformed several times and, besides this, there were numerous other attempts at a definition. This definition, however, is characteristic as an example.

This way of viewing things, however, led to very different kinds of conclusions. Hitherto attention had not been paid to the kind of connection of cause and result with their bearer. It proved to be necessary now. The doctrine of categories of Vaiśeşikam recognized two kinds of connection: conjunction (*saṃyogaḥ*) and inherence (*samavāyaḥ*). It was soon seen that this was not sufficient. Gradually the most different kinds of relationships were referred to, e.g., identity, being object, being subject, adhesion to space and time, etc.

One of the most important terms that was newly created was that of the delimiting (*avacchedakam*). Even though it was also assumed that real things are the object of an inference, it was soon recognized that one does not infer the individual thing with all its special qualities, but that one infers it according to a special property. When, for example, one infers fire from smoke, then one infers it as fire only, and nothing more. This property which determines the inferred thing as such, was called the delimiting. Thus, it was possible to combine bigger or smaller groups of things and, thus, to expand the result, and later also the cause, to specific areas whose relation to each other was to be determined. The attempts to determine the nature of the delimiting more precisely led, however, to complicated debates.

The question of absence (*abhāvaḥ*) presented special problems. The beginnings of this doctrine, so characteristic of Nyāyaḥ, go back to the time of the old school. But now it received its own features. The lack of a thing is its own total absence (*atyantābhāvaḥ*) and is characterized by the thing itself as its counterpositive (*pratiyogī*). This counterpositive is the bearer of the counterpositiveness (*pratiyogitvam*), which is not to be understood as contradictoriness (*virodhitvam*), and which is determined by a delimiting more precisely. When all things of a particular kind are lacking, then the question arose whether this is due to the sum of the single absences (*viśeṣābhāvaḥ*) or whether, besides this, there is generic absence (*sāmānyābhāvaḥ*). Often the latter was considered and it was assumed that its counterpositiveness was delimited by the respective common property. The old Nyāyaḥ had taught four kinds of absence. At the outset, together with total absence, the mutual absence (*anyonyābhāvaḥ*) of things different from one another. Whereas the first represents an essence of its own, the other belongs to the essence of these things. This absence could be easily taken into the definition of pervasion through minor alterations in the wording. The two other kinds, prior absence (*prāgabhāvaḥ*) and absence through decay (*pradhvāṃsābhāvaḥ*), presented problems. The absence of a thing, insofar as it is determined by a property that is alien to it (*vyadhikaraṇadharmāvaccchinnābhāvaḥ*), as was assumed by some - when, for example, one can say of a pot that it is absent from the standpoint of clothness - was very controversial. In this way new theories continued to be developed which led again to ever new problems and disputes. Added to all this was the exaggerated realism of the system which led to the assumption of ever new facts, e.g., when it was said that the occurrence of a thing depends on the occurrenceness (*vṛttitvam*) inherent in it. Such exaggerations could have a crippling effect ultimately and could lead everything to absurdity. And it is understandable that one largely restricted oneself to the core of the doctrine, as it was presented in common handbooks.

**2. Historical Development:**

Little is known about the beginnings of Navyanyāyaḥ because, as often happened, the earlier works were superseded by the later ones and were lost. In any case, Śivādityamiśra (c.1200) was influenced by Navyanyāyaḥ. Sondala and Taraṇimiśra, the author of a *Ratnakośaḥ*, are mentioned as important representatives of the school in the older time. However, only the *Nyāyasiddhāntadīpaḥ* by Śaśadhara is extant, who seems to have received very little attention, and Maṇikaṇṭha's *Nyāyaratnam*, towards the end of the early period.

The school reached its first climax with the great systematizer Gaṅgeśa (c.1290-1350 AD) who summarized everything achieved until then in his *Tattvacintāmaṇiḥ*. As opposed to his predecessors, Gaṅgeśa strictly limited himself to epistemology as the actual core of the system. That is why his work is divided into four books, according to the four instruments of knowledge of Nyāyaḥ: perception, inference, comparison and verbal testimony. Within this narrow framework, nonetheless, he combined all the relevant material within a clear structure with an hitherto unknown completeness. Even though in a few details the presentation of the material may not always appear satisfactory, nonetheless, as a whole his achievement was outstanding and the consequences immense. Everything significant that was later achieved, closely followed his work, i.e., in the form of writing commentaries and sub-commentaries.

Since Gaṅgeśa was so completely preoccupied with his great work, he found no time for the traditional composition of commentaries to the existing classics of the system. This void was filled by his son Vardhamāna (c.1315-1375 AD). He wrote, among others, commentaries to all the major works of Udayana and to Śrīvallabha's *Nyāyalīlāvatī*.

The generations following Gaṅgeśa did not produce anything significant. Śaṅkaramiśra (c.1405-1473), who is often mentioned, is a rather unimportant polyhistor. On the other hand, in the middle of the fifteenth century there began a lively activity by commentators. This was probably initiated by Yajñapati who wrote a commentary on the *Tattvacintāmaṇiḥ* at this time. He vigorously takes up the problems arising fom the new perspective of Navyanyāyaḥ and from the new terms that were put forward, works out the difficulties with sharpness and offers bold attempts at solutions. A line of important commentators follows him, opposing him: Jayadeva, not much younger than he, who, unlike Yajñapati, does not restrict himself to dealing with the most important problems, but who offers a continuous commentary in a concise, terse form, to which sub-commentaries were later written; further, [commentators like] Rucidatta, Pragalbha and Vāsudeva Sārvabhauma. During this period Navyanyāyaḥ, which hitherto was mainly established in Mithilā, spreads itself out into neighbouring areas. Thus, Pragalbha settles down in Benares, succeeded by his student Balabhadra and his [Balabhadra's] son, Padmanābha. And Vāsudeva transfers Navyanyāyaḥ to Bengal where, from now on, it has its main centre and from where a new direction of the school develops.

The founder of this new trend was one of Vāsudeva's students, Raghunātha Śiromaṇi (c.1480-1540). Raghunātha wrote a work *Padārthatattvanirūpaṇam* in which he examines the categories of Vaiśeṣikam from the standpoint of Navyanyāyaḥ and on the basis of the terms newly developed by it. It is said that in his work he laid the deathblow on Vaiśeṣikam. Perhaps, one can also rightly speak of a complete misunderstanding of the spirit of the old Vaiśeṣikam. In any case, in his major work, the commentary to the *Tattvacintāmaṇiḥ* called *Dīdhitiḥ*, Raghunātha relinquished the substantial questions and turned to formal problems. His chief aim here is to present indisputable definitions which may be applied to all conceivable cases; and he evolves a brilliant skill not only in forming and transforming such definitions, but also in devising the most complicated, exceptional cases which he incorporates into his definitions. This, together with his terse, and often intentionally obscure style, secured the work a decisive success; and everything important written later by the Bengal school is contained in the commentaries to Raghunātha's work. Other commentaries had also been written to the *Tattvacintāmaṇiḥ*, but they receded to the background. The most well-known among these is Mathurānātha's *Tattvacintāmaṇirahasyam* which elucidates Gaṅgeśa's work from the viewpoint of the Raghunātha school. The more generally known commentators to Raghunātha are Kṛṣṇadāsa, Bhāvananda, Jagadīśa and, most important among all, Gadādhara who died in 1703 (1709) at an unusually old age. There was some writing after him and even in the contemporary period, but they do not equal him.

In view of the great difficulty of the basic texts, simple handbooks on Navyanyāyaḥ became very popular, moreso than in the other Indian systems; these briefly present Navyanyāyaḥ epistemology, either together with the doctrine of categories, or in addition to it. The most significant of these is the *Kārikāvalī* by Viśvanātha Pañcānana (c.1580-1640), with an auto-commentary called *Siddhāntamuktāvalī*. Annam Bhaṭṭa's *Tarkasaṃgrahaḥ* and Laugākṣi Bhāskara's *Tarkakaumudī* are especially popular and wide spread.

# V.

## History of Indian Philosophy, Volume IV
## Posthumous Drafts

### Preliminary Remarks

There are several plan outlines for the complete work of the "History of Indian Philosophy" in Frauwallner's bequest.[1] The most complete of these outlines is given in Appendix C. It divides the content of the first part into three periods: the early period, the period of the systems, the aftermath. Of the sections contained in this outline Frauwallner completed the following in the two volumes already published[2]: §§1-6 in Volume I and §§7, 8, 12b in Volume II.

After the completion of the first two volumes Frauwallner had already intended a separate, fourth volume, for the presentation of Period C ("The Aftermath") of the first part ("The Philosophy of the Ancient Period").[3] This means that at this time he had already planned to divide the remaining sections of the first part into two further volumes; §§ 9-12 ("The Buddhist Systems") were intended for the third volume and §§ 13-15 for the fourth volume. The final plan of the first part is, in fact, not written down in detail anywhere, but can be inferred from the remarks already mentioned.[3] Furthermore, in the 1960s Frauwallner occasionally spoke of a "third" or "fourth volume" in this sense. It was clearly evident from his own words, however, that he no longer hoped to be able to finish more than the first part of the whole plan. The fourth volume, for which the presentations below were intended, was to have been the final volume of his "History of Indian Philosophy". Whereas Frauwallner was again able to continue work on the first part of the third volume in the last years of his life[4], he was no longer graced to take up work on the fourth volume. Nonetheless, there is a plan outline for this fourth volume and it is given in Appendix D.

Frauwallner began his work on the fourth volume in 1956, after completing his investigation of the Vinaya. This immediately resulted in a number of essays in

---

[1] BA/XI/8-12, 18-20.

[2] Salzburg: Otto Müller Verlag, 1953 and 1956. [English tr. V.M. Bedekar, Delhi: Motilal Banarsidass, 1973; repr. 1984].

[3] C/f. *Geschichte der indischen Philosophie*, Vol. 2, 1956, note 204; "Die Anfänge der indischen Logik", Anz. ÖAdW, 1956, No. 6, 98; "Mīmāṃsāsūtram" I, 1, 6-23, WZKS 5, 1961, note 7.

[4] The posthumous material to this volume are to be published separately.

which he published the detailed results of his investigation of the material.[5] This work period ended in 1961. The needs and interests of his students turned his research direction into other fields, at first to Abhidharma, and then to Navyanyāya. When upon his retirement (January 1, 1964) Frauwallner was again able to pay attention to the aims which were important to him, he first energetically took up the theme of the third volume and began with his investigation into Abhidharma and into the origin of the philosophical systems of Buddhism. This remained in the foreground till the end. Several preliminary studies were published as a consequence of these years,[6] but the presentation of the third volume itself remains a fragment,[4] and even the ever further retreating aim still to write the fourth volume remained unaccomplished. And, thus, what could be realized for this volume are only the drafts below from the years 1957-1959. Although these are fragments of the entire conception, the parts given below are in themselves largely completed presentations of a greater or smaller section of the history of Indian philosophy. They present the material, drawn directly from the sources, in a clear and descriptive form of the history of the problems, a form which always amazed us about this master of writing history of philosophy.

In these posthumous sketches we find the following parts of the whole plan (see Appendix D)[7]: the first sketch "Epistemology and Logic in the Classical Period"[8] deals with Section I. 1 ("Dialectics"), the chapter entitled "The Vāda-Handbooks" and "The Nyāyaḥ".[9]

---

[5] "Vasubandhu's Vādavidhiḥ", WZKS 1, 1957; "Die Erkenntnislehre des klassischen Sāṃkhya-Systems", WZKS 2, 1958; "Dignāga, sein Werk und seine Entwicklung", WZKS 3, 1959; "Das Eindringen der Sprachtheorie in die indischen philosophischen Systeme", Indologen-Tagung 1959, Verhandlungen, Göttingen 1960; "Sprachtheorie und Philosophie im Mahābhāṣyam des Patañjali", WZKS 4, 1960; "Mīmāṃsāsūtram I, 1, 6-23", WZKS 5, 1961.

[6] "Die Entstehung der buddhistischen Systeme", Göttingen 1971; "Abhidharma-Studien III". "Der Abhisamayavādaḥ, IV". "Der Abhidharma der anderen Schulen", WZKS 15, 1971; "Abhidharma-Studien IV: Der Abhidharma der anderen Schulen (Fortsetzung)", WZKS 16, 1972; "Abhidharma-Studien V: Der Sarvāstivādaḥ. Eine entwicklungsgeschichtliche Studie", WZKS 17, 1973.

[7] The references to the sections are based on the numbering of the plan outline given in Appendix D.

[8] This title actually refers to the entire volume. Since the introduction to the sketch is rather short and above all prepares for the subject matter, "Dialectics", it can be assumed that just as with the previous volumes, a separate, comprehensive introduction was intended for this volume as well, which would present what was unique for this epoch of Indian philosophizing and its tradition. The beginning of the sketch is dated February 7, 1957.

[9] From the brief form of the introduction to the second sketch, it can be inferred that Frauwallner also wanted to present the development of Buddhist dialectics upto Vasubandhu in the first section itself.

The second sketch "Tantrayuktayaḥ" deals with Section I. 2 ("The Scientific Systematization"). It leads from a presentation of the Tantrayuktis to the epistemology of Sāṃkhya and the achievement of the author Vṛṣagaṇa, but is interrupted after the treatment of the instruments of knowledge.[10]

The third sketch "Theory of Language" is about the entry of the theory of language into the philosophical systems[11]; after its adoption in Nyāya and Vaiśeṣika, the presentation of Mīmāṃsā follows. This sketch thus begins the section I.3 ("The Philosophy of Language"), to which the two following sketches most probably belong.[12] The fourth sketch, "Mīmāṃsā", is dated December 28, 1958 and, after the bracketed presentation of the doctrine of the eternality of sound, enters into the epistemology and the philosophical systematization of Mīmāṃsā.

The untitled, fifth sketch, dated September 6, 1959, deals with the Vṛttikāra's theory of language and, in fact, constitutes the conclusion of the presentation of the doctrine about the instruments of knowledge. Nothing is written about this itself, but the gap is filled by Frauwallner's work published in 1968, "Materialien zur ältesten Erkenntnislehre der Karmamīmāṃsā" (Materials for the Oldest Epistemology of Karmamīmāṃsā).

The sixth sketch, "Kumārila", with the introductory section dated February 10, 1959 [BA/VIII/2] and the main part April 12, 1959 [BA/VIII/5], belongs to Section I. 4 ("Mīmāṃsā").

The last, seventh sketch "Dharmakīrti" is undated and belongs to Section II. 5.

---

10 The connection to Frauwallner's essay on the epistemology of the Sāṃkhya system (see note 5 above) is evident. So the sketch must have been written in about 1957.

11 The beginninig of the sketch is dated "c. 25.1.1959". A note at the beginning of the sketch refers to the planned presentation of the theory of language in the grammar tradition. It was for the time being put in brackets, apparently because of the writing of the lecture for the Indologen-Tagung 1959 and the two articles published in 1960 and 1961 (see note 5 above), which were written concurrently.

12 Both sketches belong to the presentation of the earlier epistemology of Mīmāṃsā.

## 1. Epistemology and Logic in the Classical Period
[BA/IV/1-26]

In our presentation thus far, we have seen several times that the individual philosophical systems with which we have been dealing, gradually developed an epistemology by way of justifying their doctrines. This, however, occurred rather late, when the formation of the system itself had either reached or already passed its climax. And since schools also emerged which almost exclusively concentrated on epistemology, and since, moreover, this development was carried out under constant, mutual influence with the result that an exclusive treatment of the individual schools is impossible, it seems to be justified to deal with it [epistemology] as a separate section of the history of Indian philosophy.

It is of course obvious that the emergence of epistemolgy occurs at the end of the development which led to the formation of the major systems. The ancient philosophers very freely spoke about what they thought they had realized. Only when the different theories confronted one another and a mutual criticism began, that the question about the justification of these doctrines arose. On account of this, the question about the possibility of reliable knowledge itself gradually emerged. We can, therefore, also observe the same course in Greece. Only after the pre-Socratics presented their bold doctrines, did critical epistemolgical questions arose in Sophism. In Plato's school the way was then prepared for the development of logic, which Aristotle firmly established. In the major schools of the Hellenistic period epistemology finally becomes a strong requirement for further philosophizing. As we have seen, it was similar in India. However, despite the similarity in general, the Indian development has its own trends here as well and goes its own way.

As far as the origin of logic and epistemology is concerned, dialectics plays a special role in India. Since ancient times the spoken word was particularly important in India. One did not learn a discipline through books, but from the mouth of a teacher. And only the one who had learnt it in this way was regarded as its true authority and representative. Further, a person who wrote thought provoking works was not regarded as a great philosopher if he did not also know how to effectively present his theory and to successfully defend it in a debate with opponent views. The result was that public discussions and debates always had a significant role in the intellectual life of India since ancient times. We hear of them even in the Vedic period and there are recurring reports throughout the centuries of how great masters successfully defended their theories in public disputations and defeated their opponents. And many are said to have gone from place to place and to have celebrated their victory.

In this context the royal academies, among others, took on a special significance. One of the claims to glory, if not the duty, of Indian rulers since early times was the cultivation of literature and the sciences. In this way a circle of poets and scholars began to gather in the various courts, who assembled from time to time in order to present new works, and we can best refer to them as academies. Even here we hear of young, talented people who went from court to court so as to gain approval and donations, until a permanent position was created for them through the favour of a ruler. Such academies were, however, the ideal place for disputations. Among them was a group of experts as the assembly, and the authority of the ruler was behind the decision over victory or defeat who, apart from this, very often rewarded the winner richly. This is why the disputations in the courts is reported rather often.

With such an activity it was only natural that soon an art of debate, a dialectic, developed. It became necessary to establish the means by which a debate was to be conducted, how it was to be correctly or wrongly led and, above all, under what conditions one of the two opponents was to be declared defeated. Gradually, fixed rules for the procedure of the disputations were developed, and the Indian tendency towards systematization finally led not only to the rules being written down, but also to the details being elaborated; and, finally, proper guides and handbooks of dialectic were written.

Fortunately we can get a rather good idea of what such a guide looked like in the ancient times. We owe this to a source which we would at the outset not expect, namely, a major work on ancient Indian medicine, named after the famous physician Caraka, "Caraka's Collection" (*Carakasaṃhitā*). Upon closer consideration this is not as strange as it may first appear. Just as the works of ancient Greek medicine evince a high regard for the occupation of a physician and make far-reaching demands on his education and character, so too in ancient India it was not considered enough to impart professional knowledge to the physician, but, over and above that, a wide knowledge of a general kind was demanded of him. We therefore find valuable information about philosophical doctrines of the time in the above mentioned work.

Apart from everything else, it was also expected in a public discussion that the physician know how to present his medical skill in general as well as to effectively present his own personal views. So it is no longer amazing that a brief guide to dialectics was recorded in Caraka's work.[13]

The presentation begins with suggestions of a general kind.[14] A physician should converse with other physicians, since such a discussion (*saṃbhāṣā*) with specialists in the field instils delight in knowledge, it leads to greater clarity, it encourages the ability to express oneself, it brings respect, removes doubt, and establishes the knowledge already gained. Indeed, it can also have the effect that one, during the discussion, realizes things which one would otherwise never hear of, namely, when a discussion partner gets so carried away with the zeal of the talk, that he states things which he would otherwise keep secret.

Basically one is to distinguish between a friendly discussion (*saṃdhāya saṃbhāṣā*) and a disputation (*vigṛhya saṃbhāṣā*). In a friendly discussion one has to deal with a partner who employs understanding and knowledge together with skill in talking and arguing, and who does not confront one with anger and envy, but rather, favourably. With such a person one should speak confidently, ask questions with confidence and answer him clearly and openly, because in such a case one need not fear defeat. And one should also not look forward to inflicting defeat upon the discussion partner, nor to announce it since the entire debate is conducted in a friendly spirit.

The position is quite different in a disputation. Here one has indeed to consider one's own advantage. At the outset, one has therefore to strive to be clear with whom one is dealing and in what assembly the debate is to be conducted. The qualities that are crucial in such a debate are knowledge, understanding, good memory, presence of mind and deftness in speech. On the other hand, agitation, confusion, fear, failure of memory and inattentiveness are detrimental. In the light of these qualities one should therefore examine oneself and weigh one's abilities vis à vis the opponent, in order to see whether the opponent is superior, equally matched or inferior.

Moreover, as far as the assembly (*pariṣat*) is concerned, it is

---

[13] S. Dasgupta in his *A History of Indian Philosophy*, Cambridge, 1932, Vol. II, pp. 378-388, gives a rather detailed description of this section, though sometimes incorrect in details.

[14] CS III (Vimānasthānam) 8, 14ff.

important whether or not it possesses expert knowledge and whether it is favourable, unpartisan or hostile. If it is hostile and, moreover, does not understand the subject matter then the debate is definitely to be avoided. If, on the other hand, it is favourable, or at least unpartisan, then one may participate in the debate, even if the assembly does not have expert knowledge. One should dismiss an opponent who is insignificant and disliked, by confusing him with long speeches overlayed with quotations, by ridiculing him, by not giving him any say, by rebuking every incorrect word of his, and by such similar means. One should enter into a debate with an opponent who is superior or equally matched only if the assembly is favourable or at least non-partisan. Then, one has to consider very closely where his strength lies and what his weaknesses are. And the dialogue is to be conducted in such a way that one leads to these weak points so that the opponent is quickly and surprisingly defeated, even before he becomes conscious of it. In any case, one has to accommodate one's conduct according to the abilities of the opponent. If his knowledge is limited then one should defeat him with extensive quotations. If his memory is weak then one should attempt to confuse him with long speeches. If his power of comprehension is weak then one should embarass him by employing ambiguous talk. If he speaks with difficulty then one should object to every inadequate manner of expression, and other such methods.

Then follow a few further suggestions. But all this, even though it may give one a very lively picture of the debates and disputations of that time, would hardly have any interest for the history of Indian philosophy if Caraka had limited himself only to it. But he adds more to it, which is of great significance for the history of philosophy, because it represents the point of departure of a significant development. With the words: "One should be acquainted with the following topics in order to know how to act in disputations", he begins an enumeration of dialectical categories, i.e., a list of terms which were important for the business of debates. The list[15] covers the following terms:[16]

1. dispute (*vādaḥ*), 2. substance (*dravyam*), 3. qualities (*guṇāḥ*), 4. movement (*karma*), 5. generality (*sāmānyam*), 6. particularity (*viśeṣaḥ*), 7. inherence (*samavāyaḥ*), 8. thesis (*pratijñā*), 9. statement

[15] CS III, 8, 27-66.

[16] In my translation and interpretation of the categories I have not entirely relied on Caraka's explanations (which are in fact later than the terms handed down); I have, rather, taken the original and general meaning into consideration.

of the proof for the thesis put forward (*sthāpanā*), 10. the opposite statement of the opponent (*pratiṣṭhāpanā*), 11. reason (*hetuḥ*), 12. application (*upanayaḥ*), 13. conclusion (*nigamanam*), 14. rejoinder (*uttaram*), 15. example (*dṛṣṭāntaḥ*), 16. tenet (*siddhāntaḥ*), 17. communication (*śabdaḥ*), 18. perception (*pratyakṣam*), 19. inference (*anumānam*), 20. tradition (*aitihyam*), 21. comparison (*aupamyam*), 22. doubt (*saṃśayaḥ*), 23. the purpose one follows (*prayojanam*), 24. going astray (*savyabhicāram*), 25. inquiry or desire to know (*jijñāsā*), 26. ascertainment (*vyavasāyaḥ*), 27. presumption (*arthaprāptiḥ*), 28. the origin as a means to infer the beginning (*sambhavaḥ*), 29. the questionable (*anuyojyam*), 30. the unquestionable (*ananuyojyam*), 31. the question (*anuyogaḥ*), 32. the counter-question (*pratyanuyogaḥ*), 33. defect of speech (*vākyadoṣaḥ*), 34. excellence of speech (*vākpraśaṃsā*), 35. quibble (*chalam*), 36. fallacy (*ahetuḥ*), 37. lapse of the right time (*atītakālam*), 38. objection (*upālambhaḥ*), 39. rejection of the objection (*parihāraḥ*), 40. abandonment of the thesis (*pratijñāhāniḥ*), 41. admission of the opposite thesis (*abhyanujñā*)[17], 42. incorrect reason (*hetvantaram*), 43. missing the point (*arthāntaram*), and 44. reasons for defeat (*nigrahasthānāni*).

Explanations of each of these terms follow immediately, mainly in a few sentences, and only in a few cases somewhat more detailed.

Even a quick glance at the list makes it evident that it contains many essentials for dialectic and logic. But one immediately gets the impression of confusion in the list of what is important and what is unimportant. However, this fact is understandable if we bear in mind that we have here a phenomenon with which we often come across and which we have recognized as something typical, in fact as a law of development. We saw[18] that in the concern with a new topic in Indian philosophy one sought to master it in such a way that one gathered everything that was related to it and grouped it together, even if much of it only apparently fitted into the framework and even if the classification was merely cursory and superficial. Only afterwards an examination and sorting of the collected material was introduced, everything odd and unimportant was eliminated while at the same time one learnt to understand the essentials even better, until it was felt that

[17] A recognition of what the opponent says is also the important point included here, when one says: "You commit the same mistake", since one acknowledges the justification of the rebuke.

[18] Vol. 2, pp. 34f. [English tr. pp. 17f.].

one finally arrived at a satisfactory formulation of the topic. The same phenomenon is also here. What we find in Caraka is an ancient list of dialectical categories which contains what is important and unimportant mixed together. But here too the typical procedure of sorting and excluding what was insignificant took place, as did the deep penetration and thorough study of the essentials. However, this did not occur within the confines of the medical schools. Or rather, there is no evidence of this process in medical works. On the other hand, the decisive development occurred in a school of dialectics, namely, in the school out of which the Nyāya system later emerged. The general development of dialectics is reflected in the growth of this school. Therefore, we shall trace its progress using this example.

The later Nyāya school is recognizable to us first through a short sūtra text which afterwards became the first chapter of the Nyāyasūtra and which was already extant at the beginning of the third century AD.[19] This text contains an enumeration of dialectical categories, similar to Caraka's work, but already displays a significant progress, namely, by mentioning the following categories:

1. instruments of knowledge (*pramāṇāni*), 2. objects of knowledge (*prameyam*), 3. doubt (*saṃśayaḥ*), 4. purpose (*prayojanam*), 5. example (*dṛṣṭāntaḥ*), 6. tenet (*siddhāntaḥ*), 7. members of the argument (*avayavāḥ*), 8. deliberation (*tarkaḥ*), 9. conclusion (*nirṇayaḥ*), 10. disputation (*vādaḥ*), 11. debate (*jalpaḥ*), 12. wrangling (*vitaṇḍā*), 13. fallacious reasons (*hetvābhāsāḥ*), 14. quibble (*chalam*), 15. false objections (*jātayaḥ*), and 16. reasons for defeat (*nigrahasthānāni*).

What is immediately obvious in this list is the significantly smaller number of categories, thereby achieving more simplicity. This, however, is gained less by eliminating individual categories. To be sure, some are indeed left out: the defects and excellences of speech (nos. 33-34 in Caraka's list) are no longer included insofar as they are of a general kind and are not directly concerned with dialectics.[20] Simple terms about which there was not much to say, like the questionable and the unquestionable, the question and the counter-question

[19] It is criticized in a work by the Buddhist philosopher Nāgārjuna, which is most probably authentic, viz., a work written by Nāgārjuna himself, i.e., the *Vaidalyasūtram* (extant in a Tibetan translation P. Nos. 5626 and 5630). This fact also evinces the significance of the text.

[20] The defects enumerated by Caraka have been largely retained under the reasons for defeat.

(nos. 29-32 in Caraka's list), have been excluded. In general, the simplicity has been achieved through a better arrangement and combination of what belongs together. In his list of categories Caraka enumerates the following individually: communication (no. 17), perception (no. 18), inference (no. 19), tradition (no. 20), comparison (no. 21), presumption (no. 27), and origin (no. 28). Here, however, we find only one category which encompasses all of them, viz., the category "instruments of knowledge" (no. 1). At the beginning of Caraka's list are the following: substance, qualities, movement, generality, particularity, and inherence (nos. 2-7). These are the categories of the Vaiśeṣika system, i.e., everything out of which the world of phenomena is constituted, according to the Vaiśeṣika doctrine. Even this list is substituted by a single category here, viz., by the category "objects of knowledge" (no. 2). In this way the general character of the dialectical handbook was also retained since each school could incorporate under this title what corresponded to its own views. For this purpose the Nyāya school itself later used the categories of the ancient natural philosophy related to Vaiśeṣika.[21] We find a further combination in the category "members of the argument" (no. 7). It includes thesis, reason, application and conclusion (nos. 8 and 11-13 in Caraka's list). Finally, a number of Caraka's categories have been inserted under "reasons for defeat" (no. 16). These include: lapse of the right time (no. 37), abandonment of the thesis (no. 40), admission of the opposite thesis (no. 41)[22], incorrect reason (no. 42), and missing the point (no. 43).[23]

Apart from these summaries we also sometimes come across a division. With regard to a discussion or disputation (*vādaḥ*) Caraka said in his explanation (no. 1) that it is classified as debate (*jalpaḥ*) und wrangling (*vitaṇḍā*). Here we find all three enumerated as individual categories (nos. 10-12). Moreover, they are distinguished in the following way. A disputation is conducted with unobjectionable means, in order to establish truth and in this way to come to a decision. In a debate the concern is not with victory as regards the subject but with the person himself, and for this purpose all means are permitted. Nonetheless, here one defends a particular thesis. If, on the other hand, one

---

21 Vol. 2, pp. 71-83 [English tr. Vol. 2 pp. 46-56].

22 This may indeed be seen as identical with *matānujñā* in Nyāyaḥ.

23 Already in Caraka we find that these terms are also mentioned in the explanation of the reasons for defeat, apart from their enumeration as individual categories.

restricts oneself to defeating the opponent's thesis with all possible means, without presenting one's own position, then one is engaged in wrangling. Finally, in the new list we come across only a single category which does not appear in Caraka, viz., the category "deliberation" (no. 8), which in later times was still to play a significant role.

Nevertheless, the decisive factor which determines the picture of the list of categories, is simplicity through better classification and stricter combination. With this great progress was achieved. What was superfluous was on the whole eliminated and what was important was brought forward. Nyāya therefore retained this list continuously and it lies at the basis of the fully developed Nyāya system.

However, the development was not restricted merely to sorting out and simplifying the category list. Much more significant was the reflection on and the elaboration of the individual terms. A beginning had already been made by Caraka, viz., in the explanations of the category list. Each of the categories was here described and classified. And in some cases even Nyāya did not, or hardly, go beyond what we already find mentioned by Caraka. Thus, Caraka explains "example" (no. 15) as something about which both the expert and the layman have the same opinion. The same explanation, in practically the same words, is repeated by Nyāya. Caraka explains "tenet" (no. 16) as a sentence put forward as certain, having been tested over and over again by experts and proved with reasons. He distinguishes four kinds: tenets that apply to all systems (*sarvatantrasiddhāntaḥ*), tenets which are unique to a particular system (*pratitantrasiddhāntaḥ*), tenets that have validity for a particular problem (*adhikaraṇasiddhāntaḥ*), and tenets which are regarded by the participants of a disputation as proved (*abhyupagamasiddhāntaḥ*). The same classification is also valid for Nyāya. In the case of a quibble (no. 35) we come across a further feature. Here Caraka had distinguished between a "quibble with reference to a word" (*vākchalam*) - when one imputes another sense to a word used by the opponent, and between a "quibble with reference to generality" (*sāmānyacchalam*) - when one generalises an expression of the opponent in an inadmissable way. Nyāya adds to this "quibble with reference to a metaphor" (*upacāracchalam*) - when one deliberately takes an expression intended metaphorically in a literal way. But his is a minor addition. In general, however, there was not much to say about such terms. The emphasis was on other categories, on account of which the decisive development occurred, viz., the instruments of valid knowledge (*pramāṇāni*), the members of the argument (*avayavāḥ*), fallacious reasons (*hetvābhāsāḥ*), false objections (*jātayaḥ*), and reasons for defeat (*nigrahasthānāni*). We shall therefore consider these now.

In the ancient period the role which the instruments of valid knowledge (*pramāṇāni*) plays was relatively insignificant. As we have already said, Caraka had enumerated several such instruments, whereas Nyāya substituted for them the single category "instruments of valid knowledge". Within this category it distiguished four such instruments: sense perception (*pratyakṣam*), inference (*anumānam*), communication (*śabdaḥ*), and comparison (*upamānam*), whereas Caraka listed several others over and above these. Thus, not only was what belonged together combined, but it was also sorted and the superfluous eliminated. As for the rest, in the ancient period one limited oneself to giving short explanations to each of the instruments of valid knowledge. This category was given greater significance later and in another context. We shall therefore return to this point in more detail below.

Even in early times the second category mentioned above was dealt with in thorough detail, viz., the members of the argument (*avayavāḥ*). We too should go into it closely, since it developed more and more as the core of dialectics. The development proceded more or less in the following way. It was natural, at the outset, that the ancient handbooks on dialectics also enumerated what aided an argument under each of the dialectical categories. Thus, we find in Caraka several such categories mentioned and briefly explained. The most important of these are thesis (*pratijñā*), and reason (*hetuḥ*). Their meaning is clear. They are concerned with the basic presentation of one's own thesis and the reason for it, at each disputation. The explanation given under "thesis" is accordingly simple. It was defined as a presentation of the probandum (*sādhyanirdeśaḥ*, etc.) or as the formulation of one's own thesis (*pakṣavacanam*). Even in later times this explanation was not altered. The attempt to define "reason", however, proceeded further. Caraka had said: "The reason is the origin of knowledge (*upalabdhikāraṇam*), namely, sense perception, inference, communication, and comparison; since what is known through these causes, is fact".[24] This formulation was not satisfactory. Above all, it does not mention that the reason is one of the members of the disputation. It was improved in the

---

[24] CS III 8, 33; with Caraka one often finds ancient formulations together with later ones; I am giving the ancient ones here.

sense that one stated the point to the effect that the reason is a logical explanation (*yuktivādaḥ*) based on sense perception, inference or trustworthy testimony.[25] In any case the reason was at the outset seen as a detailed justification of one's own thesis, which rested on the instruments of valid knowledge. However, this definition was soon to be surpassed.

To the two members of the argument mentioned above a third, viz., an example (*dṛṣṭāntaḥ*), was very early attached. In this context Caraka had said that an example is something about which both the expert and the layman have the same opinion and which is, therefore, ideal to explain what is to be explained.[26] He understood it as a clear, recognized case which one referred to in order to clarify one's thesis and reason. To present such examples in a disputaion was a matter of course and was certainly current practice since ancient times. The example was given real significance, however, only in cases in which the thesis and the reason were not presented in the form of a detailed argument, but rather as a simple conclusion. In such cases it could thereby serve to establish the connection between the cause and the result, and, indeed, it was used for this purpose. Let us take as an example an inference which is often repeated as a typical example in Indian logic, viz., the argument to prove the transitoriness of sound (*śabdaḥ*). It is directed against the Mīmāṃsā doctrine according to which sound as a quality of ether is eternal, which therefore should prove the eternality of the Veda.[27] It was said: Sound is transitory because it is caused. The thesis here is: sound is transitory; and the reason for it is: because it is caused. Now, in order to show that something caused is really transitory, an example of a transitory object, like a pot, was given and it was said: A pot is caused and is also transitory; therefore, sound too, which is also caused, must be transitory. In this way, an example became an important, in fact a necessary, member of the proof. At the same time the thesis and the reason obtained a narrower meaning.[28] Thus, it was no longer understood as detailed

---

[25] C/f. *Yogācārabhūmiḥ;* c/f. also AS 105, 5f.

[26] CS III 8, 36; Caraka recognizes only this example (not *udāharaṇam*!), but includes it with *sthāpanā* and *pratiṣṭhāpanā* under the members of the proof.

[27] See below pp. 110ff., p. 114.

[28] It received the name *udāharaṇam.* The connection with the old *dṛṣṭāntaḥ* is indicated in places like NBh. on V, 1, 6.

presentations of one's own view, but as members of an argument. They retained this meaning even in later times because it was in the form of the inference that the theory of proof was continued and developed. A possibility was seen here to go beyond a mere presentation and explanation of categories so as to achieve a strict, methodical procedure of proof.

One of the next steps for this was that the members of the proof were increased. Initially, there were three members: the thesis, sound is transitory; the reason, because it is caused; and the example, what is caused is transitory, as we see it in the case of a pot. In presentations within the framework of a disputation, which were either to convince or defeat an opponent, it was now desireable to expressly draw the conclusion from the knowledge obtained through the example. This was done by supplying two further members in addition to the existing three. To the example: what is caused is transitory, like a pot, was added: sound is caused, therefore it is transitory. The first statement "sound is caused" was called application (*upanayaḥ*); the second "therefore it is transitory", the conclusion (*nigamanam*). Thus, one obtained a five membered scheme for the proof.

A further step in the improvement of this scheme was the following. Just as one showed by example that in the presence of the cause the result obtains, so too could one show by a counter-example that the absence of one entails the absence of the other. Thus, if one wants to prove the transitoriness of sound one may take the soul as a counter-example and say: what is not caused is also not transitory, as we see it in the case of the soul; sound, on the contrary, is caused, therefore it is transitory. Accordingly, two kinds of examples were distinguished: examples of similarity, and examples of dissimilarity. Examples of dissimilarity could be important if a similar example were not to be found. Sometimes the view was adopted that for the sake of completeness and certainty of a conclusion both examples were necessary.

In this way a fixed form of the argument was created, which appeared to make a reliable proof possible. Nevertheless, this success led to the attempt to further elaborate the five membered scheme of the inference and to add other members to it. This was done in the following way. It was said that at first there is the desire to know something (*jijñāsā*). The starting point for this inquiry was a doubt (*saṃśayaḥ*) concerning any object. The effort to remove the doubt was made only if a purpose (*prayojanam*) was associated with it, and only if there was a possibility to fulfil the aim (*śakyaprāptiḥ*). Only afterwards can a removal of the doubt (*saṃśayavyudāsaḥ*) follow. When these five steps have been taken then the members of the argument already mentioned follow.

The expansion of the five membered method of proof was not a happy one and was generally rejected. Or, it was said, the five new members are of a different kind and should rather be separated from the proof. This was the way suggested by Sāṃkhya. According to it the five new members do not belong to the scheme of the proof but are an aid to a systematic investigation of the object. They are means of explanation (*vyākhyāṅgam*), whereas the remaining five are means by which to teach others (*parapratipādanāṅgam*).[29] Largely, however, the new members were completely rejected. Even Nyāya decided to do this and set up the five membered scheme of proof in the Sūtras.

Not only was a definite form of the proof created with the establishing of the fivefold scheme, but an insight was already achieved through it into the conditions on which the inference depended. At first it was seen that there was some object at the basis of a conclusion, like the transitoriness of sound, which had two qualities (*dharmāḥ*). One quality is the probans (*sādhanadharmaḥ*) and the other is the probandum (*sādhyadharmaḥ*). The possibility of the conclusion is based on the fact that both these qualities emerge as connected to each other. And this connection was shown by the example. In the conclusion about the transitoriness of sound the locus of both qualities (*dharmī*) is sound. The probandum is transitoriness, and the proving quality is that of being caused. The object that served as an example is one in which both the qualities of being caused and of being transitory appear together, as with a pot.

On the basis of this knowledge the doctrine of the members of the proof was given the following form in the Nyāyasūtras (NSū I, 1, 32-39): "The members of the proof are thesis, reason, instance[30], application and conclusion. The thesis (*pratijñā*) is the presentation of the probandum. The reason (*hetuḥ*) is what demonstrates the probandum

---

[29] YD 47, 20-22; for different kinds of methodical schemes see W. Ruben, *Die Nyāyasūtra's*, Leipzig, 1928, note 76.

[30] The Nyāyasūtras choose this expression in order to distinguish the example in a conclusion from an example in general, which constitutes a further category in the text.

on the basis of its similarity to the instance cited, or on the basis of its dissimilarity. The instance (*udāharaṇam*) is an example which, on the basis of its similarity to the probandum[31], bears its qualities - or the contrary on the basis of its counter example. The application (*upanayaḥ*) is the use, in the light of the cited instance, of the probandum, when one says: it is the same in this case, or it is not so. The conclusion (*nigamanam*) is a repetition of the thesis with reference to the reason."

With this arrangement of the doctrine of argumentation a first end was achieved. The inadequacy of the method of argument contained in it is evident. It depends above all merely on analogy conclusions, the deficiency of which had to be evident repeatedly. But for a beginning the inherent achievement cannot be underestimated. And at least a useful starting point was provided for a further development of the theory of inference.

The next important category were the fallacious reasons (*hetvābhāsāḥ*). We find these even in Caraka under the name false reasons (*ahetavaḥ*), since, from the earliest times, the textbooks on dialectics presented, together with the terms and rules, the respective errors that could be committed. The Nyāyasūtras acknowledge five such fallacies: of going astray (*savyabhicārī*), of being contradictory (*viruddhaḥ*), of theme similarity (*prakaraṇasamaḥ*), of being related to the probandum (*sādhyasamaḥ*), and of the mistimed (*kālātītaḥ*).[32]

A fallacy of going astray (*savyabhicārī hetvābhāsaḥ*) is explained as what is not exclusive (*anaikāntikaḥ*), i.e., a reason that is not compelling.[33] Assuming someone wants to prove the eternality of sound by saying that it cannot be felt (*asparśatvam*), then he can cite the soul as an example, which also cannot be felt and which is eternal. However, against this it may be objected that there are other examples which indeed cannot be felt, but which are not eternal as, for instance, the intellect (*buddhiḥ*) which according to the Vaiśeṣika and Nyāya doctrine is a quality of the soul and is transitory. The same is the case with a counter example. A pot can be cited, which can be felt and is not eternal. Other counter examples, however, can be felt and are at the same time eternal, as with atoms which in fact have the quality of

---

31 Here the quality of the probandum is not meant, but the object connected with it.

32 NSū I, 2, 4-9.

33 This and the following explanations are according to the Nyāyabhāṣyam.

touchability, but which in Vaiśeṣika and Nyāya are regarded as eternal. Thus, the cited reason, untouchability, is in the examples not exclusively connected with the desired conclusion, and the same is valid for the counter examples. It is therefore not compelling and is to be regarded as a fallacy that goes astray.

A contradictory fallacy (*viruddho hetvābhāsaḥ*) is one which contradicts a tenet which one has already iterated. The following case is given as an example. An old sentence in the classical Sāṃkhya system, which was to explain becoming and disappearance in the phenomenal world, was: "This threefold world disappears from sight because it has been taught that the world is not eternal. However, it also exists after its disappearance because it has been taught that the world is not destroyed".[34] A contradiction was believed to have been found between the non-eternality of the phenomenal world given as a reason, and the tenet immediately following it, i.e., that it exists after its disappearance. The disappearance was explained as a relinquishing of its own nature and was thus seen as a complete destruction, which of course contradicts the Sāṃkhya view of a continued existence of all things.

A fallacy having theme similarity (*prakaraṇasamo hetvābhāsaḥ*) obtains when what gave rise to the discussion is presented as a reason. In the case of sound, for example, clear signs of transitoriness or eternality are not evident, and precisely this was the occasion for the whole argument about its transitoriness or eternality. If one makes the inference: Sound is not eternal because no sign of eternality is perceivable in it, as in the case of ether, then he commits the error of a fallacy having theme similarity.

The fallacy of being related to the probandum (*sādhyasamo hetvābhāsaḥ*) is a reason which is not different from what is to be proved insofar as it first requires to be proved itself. As an example the following conclusion is generally given: shadow is a substance because it moves. The point here is: in the beginnings of natural philosophy shadow was largely considered as something essential, justified by the fact that it moves.[35] However, according to the Vaiśeṣika view, which Nyāya follows, to move implies the existence of the category movement in the substance which is its locus. So shadow would really be a substance if movement of such a kind were present. But this needs to

---

[34] See Vol. I, p. 352 [English tr. p. 277].

[35] See Vol. II, p. 38 [English tr. p. 20].

be proved first, since the apparent movement may depend on the light interrupted by a moving object. Therefore, the reason is still in need of proof, as the thesis itself. Hence, in the given example there is the fallacy related to the probandum.

A mistimed fallacy (*kālātīto hetvābhāsaḥ*) was originally understood as a reason which was not given at the right time during a disputation, i.e., not at the correct place.[36] Later, this presentation of the reason in the wrong place was counted as one of the reasons for defeat and was therefore given another artificial explanation. It was said: when one argues "sound is eternal because it is made manifest through contact, as in the case of form (*rūpam*)", then the situation is the following. The form, which in darkness is made manifest through the light of a lamp, is existent both before and after, and is only made manifest by light. The same is true according to Mīmāṃsā for sound as well. It too exists always and is only made manifest by beating the drum with a drumstick. However, whereas form is made manifest immediately the ray of light is in contact with its bearer, in the case of sound the manifestation is later, because one hears it only after the contact of the stick with the drum has past - and especially when the hearer is a distance away. Therefore, as far as the relation with time is concerned, the reason does not concur with the example exactly. Thus, there obtains a mistimed fallacy.

The next two categories, false objections (*jātayaḥ*) and reasons for defeat (*nigrahasthānāni*), occupy a significantly greater position in the Nyāyasūtras than the fallacies, so much so that they take up an entire chapter. After a brief explanation in the first chapter these two categories are again dealt with in the fifth, moreover in detail in all their varieties.

If we inquire into the reasons for this strong emphasis then they may well be the following. As already said, the theory of argumentation more and more came to be the core of dialectics. We saw in this context that, despite the good beginnings, one did not at the outset go beyond the presentation of a conclusion based on simple analogies, and this stagnant point was not overcome for a long time. This means that there were often presentations of false analogy-conclusions in the disputations, without being in a position to recognize and demonstrate the errors clearly. Because of this the significance of the two mentioned

---

36 CS III 8, 58; c/f. NBh 84, 13ff. on NSū I, 2, 9.

categories began to grow in importance. Under these circumstances it could have easily happened, initially, that an opponent put forth objections which indeed one found to be incorrect, but which could not be refuted immediately because the rules of argument had not yet been recognized. Obviously, one strove, at least afterwards, to detect and to refute the errors, in order to be armed against similar cases. These objections together with all their refutations were then put together and, thus, a long list of false objections (*jātayaḥ*) emerged. It occupies the first half of the fifth chapter and its origin is indebted to the apparent unpleasant experiences at the disputations.

As far as the reasons for defeat (*nigrahasthānāni*) are concerned, these played an important role all along, since it was always of crucial significance in a disputation according to what principles victory and defeat were decided. But even in the preparation of these rules it must have been of great consequence that one was not in a position to demonstrate the errors of the argument unequivocally. The result of this was that the superficial errors, which one may have incurred in the disputation, came to the foreground and were dealt with in detail. And this gave rise to a large number of reasons for defeat, which makes up the second half of the fifth chapter.

If it is now understandable why these categories take up so much space in the Nyāyasūtras then, on account of their technically minor importance, they should be dealt with and explained here only briefly. Suffice it to show on the basis of a few examples how these categories were interpreted and expounded.

To begin with the false objections (*jātayaḥ*): under the circumstances described above the most obvious thing that one had to consider was that against a given argument the opponent answered with another conclusion based on analogy, which proved the opposite. In this case the opponent's argument, as well as one's own, was based on an example of similarity, or of dissimilarity. Accordingly, for the first two kinds of false objections the corresponding rejoinders to one's own proof were taught, which used such similarities or dissimilarities, and it was said[37]: "A corresponding rejoinder on the basis of similarity or dissimilarity (*sādharmyavaidharmyasamau*)[38] obtains when a proof is

[37] NSū V, 1, 2.

[38] To names with *-samaḥ*, *pratiṣedhaḥ* is to be added, which is generally omitted.

supplied on the basis of similarity or dissimilarity and the contrary of the property one wants to prove is possible." The following cases were cited by way of example. Assuming the argument is about whether the soul is mobile or not,[39] one can assert the following inference in order to prove its mobility: "The soul is mobile because it possesses the qualities which produce movement of a substance. A lump of earth possesses these qualities and is mobile. The soul too possess them. Therefore, it is mobile." The opponent may answer this with the following argument: "Ether, for example, which is ubiquitous, is immobile. And since the soul is also ubiquitous, it is immobile." Both these inferences are based on the similarity of the examples. Thus, there obtains a rejoinder on the basis of similarity of examples (*sādharmyasamaḥ pratiṣedhaḥ*). One's own proof could in exactly the same way be based on dissimilarity, as can the opponent's.

Such antagonistic objections were difficult to refute under the conditions of the doctrine of proof at that time, since there was a lack of criteria by which to decide whether one's own example or that of the opponent's was convincing, i.e., whether in the case mentioned the mobility of the soul is proved by the similarity to a lump of earth, or that its immobility is proved by the similarity to ether. Therefore, the attempts which were made to master these difficulties were for the time being inadequate. At the outset it was said that not every arbitrary quality is appropriate to justify what is to be proved. One could not, for instance, infer "cow" simply from "being horned", but only from the general character of cow-ness.[40] This was later expressed more precisely. It was said that it is inadmissable to infer one quality from another merely because both obtain in one example together, but only when it is decided on the basis of the example that both qualities stand in a relation to each other as cause and effect.[41] But exactly wherein this relation lies, was not possible to say. Thus, the attempts to refute especially the most important kinds of false objections, remained unsatisfactory at first.

Together with these kinds of false objections, which were based on the fundamental doubtfulness of all conclusions by analogy, others

---

[39] By mobility is meant here change of place, in exactly the sense in which the Nyāya examples generally presuppose the Vaiśeṣika views.

[40] NSū V, 1, 3; c/f. VSū III, 1, 17.

[41] NBh to sūtram I, 1, 39 (64, 12-16).

were enumerated in an attempt to change and, thereby, to render invalid, the original analogy through auxiliary conditions. To these belong, for example, the corresponding rejoinders based on reasons of excess or deficiency (*utkarṣāpakarṣasamau pratiṣedhau*) or on grounds of alternatives (*vikalpasamaḥ*).[42] The corresponding rejoinder based on reasons of excess indicates that the object compared possesses a further quality which is lacking in the object of the conclusion, and maintains that the cited similarity is therefore inadequate to infer the desired conclusion. In the inference referred to above, viz., that the soul is mobile because, as with a lump of earth, it possesses the qualities which cause movement in a substance, the opponent objects, for instance, that the lump of earth moreover has the quality of touchability, which lacks in a soul, and maintains that one is not justified to infer mobility in the case of a soul on grounds of its similarity to a lump of earth. The corresponding rejoinder to this on grounds of deficiency constitutes the antithesis. It is based on the point that the object compared lacks a quality which the object of the conclusion possesses and, on the basis of this, disputes the validity of the cited analogy conclusion. Such a rejoinder thus obtains when, with the conclusion under discussion, an opponent explains that the soul is ubiquitous whereas the lump of earth lacks this quality, and that the conclusion from the similarity to a lump of earth is inadmissable. The corresponding rejoinder based on various possibilities finally assumes that, in the objects which are compared, the proving quality can be connected with the most various, mutually opposing qualites. Thus, for example, objects which possess the qualities which cause movement in a substance could be partly light and partly heavy. It was said, however, that it is just as well possible that the proving quality, together with the quality yet to be proved, can also appear together with its opposite, viz., that the mentioned objects could be partly mobile and partly static. Thus, the conclusion about the mobility of a substance from the presence of qualities which cause its movement, is not decisive.

The rejoinder to all these objections implies that for the correctness of an inference a complete concurrence between the object of the conclusion and the example is not necessary, but that even a partial agreement is sufficient. Thus, in the epistemological instrument of comparison (*upamānam*) a certain similarity between the compared things

---

42 NSū V, 1, 4-6.

suffices. Thus, when the proving quality is given in the object of the conclusion and in the example, and its relation to the quality yet to be proved is established in the example, a dissimilarity to other qualities cannot, to the contrary, be made valid.

To these false objections, all of which are due to the deficiency of the analogy inference, a series of further sophisms of the most various kinds were then listed, which could be presented at disputations and despite their threadbareness could be baffling at first sight. Suffice it to give one or two examples of these.

One group is made up by the respective rejoinders based on contiguity and non-contiguity (*prāptyaprāptisamau*).[43] These lie in the fact that the opponent says: a reason can prove what is to be proved depending on whether the reason is contiguous to it or not. If it is contiguous then there is no longer any difference between the two which are in contact with each other, as between the water of a river and that of the sea, as soon as the river flows into the sea. The reason is therefore no longer the reason. If, on the other hand, the reason is not contiguous to what is to be proved then the reason cannot prove it, just as the light of a lamp cannot illuminate an object not contiguous to it. In rejecting this it was said that, on the one hand, a cause can indeed bring about its effect through contiguity whithout losing its character as a cause, just as a potter is in contact with clay through his tools when making a pot. On the other hand, an effect without contiguity is also possible as, for example, by magic.

Another sophistic objection is the corresponding rejoinder by reason of being not produced (*anutpattisamaḥ*).[44] This has the following form. The inference is made: clay is transitory because it is created through contiguity, like a pot. The opponent replies: before the production of clay, i.e., in the case of unoriginated clay, the being-produced through contiguity, which justifies its transitoriness, is not given. Consequently, there is no transitoriness and, hence its eternality follows. However, whatever is eternal, cannot originate. This objection was refuted by the remark that before its production clay is non-existent and no decision at all can apply to something not present. On the other hand, no sooner it exists than it is present through some effort and, therefore, its transitoriness follows.

---

[43] NSū V, 1, 7-8.

[44] NSū V, 1, 12-13.

So much for the false objections. As far as the reasons for defeat (*nigrahasthānāni*) are concerned, these, as we have already said, belong to one of the most important dialectical categories since ancient times - since it was always of decisive importance on what basis victory and defeat in a disputation should be judged. We therefore already find a long list by Caraka. The number is increased in the Nyāyasūtras and covers cases of the most various kinds.

Accordingly, the incompetence of a debater, irrespective of the thesis he is defending, can lead to his disqualification and, thereby, to his defeat. Such an incompetence obtains when, despite repeating it three times, he is still not in a position to understand the opponent's statement, although it is intelligible to the assembly (*ajñānam*). Further, when his memory fails him, viz., when he is not able to repeat the opponent's thesis (*ananubhāṣaṇam*), or when no answer to the opponent's charges dawns on him (*apratibhā*).

Moreover, a debater is to be declared as defeated when he is incapable of leading a disputation in an appropriate manner, or when he utters anything meaningless (*nirarthakam*), unconnected (*apārthakam*), ununderstandable (*avijñātārtham*), or not related to the subject (*arthāntaram*), or when he unnecessarily repeats himself (*punaruktam*).

The technical errors which lead to a debater's defeat are particularly important. These are deficient argument and incorrect refutation of the opponent. An argument is deficient when the members of its proof are incomplete (*nyūnam*), or when superfluous members are supplied (*adhikam*); further, when the members are not presented in the correct sequence (*aprāptakālam*). It is, above all, a great blunder to put forward fallacious reasons (*hetvābhāsāḥ*). The errors of refutations consist, further in overlooking the mistakes of the opponent (*paryanuyojyopekṣaṇam*), or in finding fault with something that is not erroneous (*niranuyojyānuyogah*).

Finally, the defeat of a debater is unambiguously decided when he himself renounces his own thesis. This can occur when he implicitly drops his thesis (*pratijñāhāniḥ*) and proceeds towards another thesis (*pratijñāntaram*) and to another reason (*hetvantaram*). But it can also be the case that he contradicts his original thesis (*pratijñāvirodhaḥ*) or expressly surrenders it (*pratijñāsaṃnyāsaḥ*).[45]

These are essentially the reasons for defeat as taught in the Nyāya-sūtras. The ideas on which they are based are clear and rational. They therefore continued to gain importance and Nyāya itself adhered to them always. Their weakness lies in the fact that the errors which are concerned with the core of the disputation, viz., the proof, are inadequately dealt with. What is given are, together with superficial errors of form, only inadequately grounded fallacies which were, therefore, later vehemently disputed. But the reason, as already mentioned, was due to the inadequacies of the doctrine of proof at that time, because what constituted a secure proof had not then been recognized.

With the organization of the doctrine of false objections and the reasons for defeat dealt with above, the development of dialectics in early Nyāya was complete.

---

[45] I am not considering the evidently later explanations of these reasons for defeat related to the theory of inference based on analogy.

## 2. Tantrayuktayaḥ
## [BA/IV/44-49]

(With Vasubandhu the development of dialectics reached a climax and at the same time a concluding point, since Dignāga immediately follows Vasubandu and he [Dignāga] founded the logico-epistemological school of Buddhism. And Dignāga did not only develop dialectics even further. Much more, he drew encouragement from the most varied sources, in order to combine everything into a great edifice of a universal epistemology. Before proceeding on to Dignāga we, therefore, also have to trace the other developments which he resumes. The most important among them is the scientific systematization.)

With regard to this the situation is the following. When systematic textbooks for the different branches of knowledge began to be written in India, a genuine Indian urge toward systematization was also stirred, i.e., rules began to be laid down how such textbooks were to be written *(tantrayuktayaḥ)* since, it was said, these rules illuminate the topic to be communicated, like the sun lights up a forest of lotuses, and a lamp a home. And whoever trains his reason in a scientific work on the basis of these rules, will easily come to understand other works. If, on the other hand, one studies such works without knowing these rules then one will not grasp their meaning. Incorrectly understood doctrines only cause injury, just as a weapon harms the person who does not know how to wield it, whereas it helps and protects an expert.[46]

Such rules for the composition of textbooks are of course generally valid and not limited to the specific disciplines, especially not to philosophy. It is for this reason that we do not find the oldest, extant collections of such rules in a philosophical work, but rather in a textbook on polity, in Kauṭilya's *Arthaśāstram*, and in a work on medicine, Suśruta's *Saṃhitā*.[47] The manner in which the composition of these works was undertaken and further improved is similar to that of the composition of the dialectical categories, as we have already seen it as being typical. We can therefore be brief in the following, all the more so because only the later development has any philosophical significance.

Here too the beginning consists of a widest possible collection of the relevant material. That is why we find in both Kauṭilya and Suśruta a long list put together - 32 in all for each - of terms and rules which are to be taken in consideration when compiling textbooks. Brief explanations are given in each case and the application elucidated with

---

46 CS XII, 75-78; c/f. *Suśrutasaṃhitā*, Uttaratantram 65, 3.

47 *Kauṭalīyam Arthaśāstram* XV and *Suśrutasaṃhitā*, Uttaratantram 65.

examples from their own respective works. A few examples will give a sufficient idea of the treatment of the material.[48]

In the first place is the topic *(adhikaraṇam)*. It is what the presentation of the textbook in question is concerned with. Then follows the order *(vidhānam)*, by which is meant the sequence of each of the sections. Combination *(yogaḥ)* is the connection among the parts of a sentence which belong together. An enunciation *(uddeśaḥ)* is a summary mention [of the subject]. A declaration *(nirdeśaḥ)* is a detailed explanation. An indication *(atideśaḥ)* is a justification through what has already been stated. A reference *(pradeśaḥ)* is a justification through what has yet to be stated. A comparison *(upamāna)* is an explanation of what is not seen through what is seen. An instance *(nirdarśanam)* refers to a justification of something through an example. Doubt *(saṃśayaḥ)* is expressed when there are two opposing justifications in one case. A theory of another which one does not contradict is regarded as approved *(anumatam)*. One's own terminology *(svasaṃjñā)* is understood to refer to terms one does not hold in common with other systems, etc.

Suffice it to randomly select a few of these examples in order to give an idea of what was understood by the rules of compiling textbooks *(tantrayuktayaḥ)* in early times and how they were explained. The further development took place in the known manner again, in the sense of an advanced examination and simplification of the material which was collected initially rather arbitrarily. We can already trace this development in fact on philosophical grounds, even if it is at a far advanced stage. The rules for the composition of textbooks were adopted, and further evolved by the Sāṃkhya system; this was done in the following way.[49]

At the outset, we find a significantly fewer number of rules. Only eleven are enumerated and discussed. Others are merely referred to briefly. The explanations given are generally retained in the previous form. Some are grasped more clearly and, sporadically, they also evince an intellectual progress. What is important above all is that, beyond this, a few new terms and rules are added. These include instruments of valid knowledge *(pramāṇāni)* and the members of the proof *(avaya-*

---

[48] S. Dasgupta supplies a complete list, loc.cit., pp. 389-392.

[49] These are dealt with in the only detailed work that is extant from the classical period of the system, viz., in *Yuktidīpikā*, 2-6.

*vāḥ),* which we have already come across under the dialectical categories. Thereby, a complete turning point in the development is heralded.

The traditional terms and rules for compiling textbooks had in view essentially the style of the material, i.e., the outer form. The instruments of valid knowledge and the members of the proof, on the other hand, are concerned with the content. They are to prove the presented doctrines and thus give them a firm foundation. This, however, means a significant shift of interests. Through this, the rules for the composition of textbooks acquired quite a new and unexpected importance, in fact, above all for the philosophical systems. That is why the development continues from here. The person, however, who led to it was the great Sāṃkhya teacher Vṛṣagaṇa.

We have already spoken about Vṛṣagaṇa in the presentation of the Sāṃkhya system.[50] We have seen him as one of the most important representatives of the system, who introduced a far-reaching transformation of it, namely, through the creation of the system of 60 principles *(Ṣaṣṭitantram)* and through a work of the same name in which he presented it. The system of the 60 principles encompasses 50 terms *(pratyayāḥ)* and ten basic teachings *(mūlikārthāḥ).* We can ignore the 50 terms here, since they are merely concerned with Sāṃkhya psychology. The ten basic teachings, however, are more important for our context. In them Vṛṣagaṇa precisely dealt with the fundamental terms of the system and brought them into clear relation. Indeed, he did not thereby create anything new, but he found a new systematic form for the traditional doctrines. This corresponded to the spirit of the conventional rules for the composition of textbooks *(tantrayuktayaḥ).* He could therefore quite rightly call his work such a textbook *(tantram),* since it followed these rules in its structure.[51] However, he also adhered to the rules newly adopted by Sāṃkhya, rules which had the aim of establishing the presented doctrine. He attempted, thereby, to substantiate his ten basic teachings in a strict, systematic way with the help of the instruments of valid knowledge and the members of the proof. For this purpose he presented the instruments of valid knowledge at the beginning of his work in order then, by means of them, to derive each of the fundamental teachings. Perhaps, what is most significant and unique in

---

[50] Vol. 1, pp. 319ff. [English tr. pp. 251ff.].

[51] What the *Yuktidīpikā* says about the application of these rules in the *Sāṃkhyakārikā*, we may also regard as valid for Vṛṣagaṇa's work.

his philosophical achievement lies in this section of this work. Before proceeding on to a presentation and assessment of this accomplishment we need first to consider the material at his disposal, i.e., we have to consider the level reached in his time by the doctrine of the instruments of valid knowledge and of the members of the proof.

We can continue from what we have already stated, because we came across both the instruments of valid knowledge and the members of the proof in the context of the dialectical categories – as indeed some terms in handbooks on dialectics are common with rules for the composition of textbooks. We have already discussed the members of the proof in detail and we may therefore be brief here. Sāṃkhya acknowledges in an old fashioned way ten members of a proof: the desire to know something *(jijñāsā)*, doubt *(saṃśayaḥ)*, purpose *(prayojanam)*, the possibility to fulfil the aim *(śakyaprāptiḥ)*, removal of the doubt *(saṃśayavyudāsaḥ)*, thesis *(pratijñā)*, reason *(hetuḥ)*, example *(dṛṣṭāntaḥ)*, application *(upasaṃhāraḥ)*, and conclusion *(nigamanam)*. These ten were divided into two groups. It was said that the first five, the desire to know *(jijñāsā)*, etc., serve as an explanation for the topic concerned *(vyākhyāṅgam)*. The last five, thesis, etc., serve to teach others *(parapratipādanāṅgam)*. We have yet to consider how these members of the proof were brought into relation with the instruments of valid knowledge.

There is much more to say about the instruments of valid knowledge themselves. For this we have go further back in time.

Instruments of valid knowledge were already mentioned in the oldest textbooks on dialectics. Initially, they were enumerated individually, as with Caraka. They were later grouped together under the name "instruments of valid knowledge" *(pramāṇāni)*. At first there were a large number of them, because the well-known phenomenon applies here too, namely, at the beginning to enumerate everything that somehow appeared to belong together. Thus, as instruments of valid knowledge we find not only perception *(pratyakṣam)* and inference *(anumānam)* mentioned, but also communication *(śabdaḥ)*, comparison *(upamānam)*, analogous conclusion *(arthāpattiḥ)*, absence *(abhāvaḥ)*, or non-perception *(anupalabdhiḥ)*, origin *(saṃbhavaḥ)*, tradition *(aitihyam)*, presentiment *(pratibhā)* and several other similar ones.[52] Soon

[52] In the translation of the terms I am also taking into consideration, above all, the oldest explanations by Caraka.

one began to sort these as well and to eliminate what did not strictly come into consideration as an instrument of valid knowledge. This applied particularly to origin, tradition, and the like. With the other instruments of valid knowledge the different philosophical schools saw the matter differently. We can say, in general, that those schools which very early decided on a definite number, accepted more instruments of knowledge than the others. Hence, Nyāya acknowledges four: perception, inference, communication and comparison; Mīmāṃsā six, adding to this list analogous conclusion and absence. Perception and inference were generally accepted. Communication was accepted by those schools which took recourse to revelation or, at least, considered it valid, because revelation counted as communication.

## 3. Theory of Language
[BA/VII/1-32]

(The theory of language of the grammarians may have been developed thus far, before it was taken over by the philosophical systems. We shall now turn to them.)

The ways in which the theories of language found an entry into philosophy were different. One of the first and most important ways was the following. Among the instruments of valid knowledge enumerated in the old textbooks on dialectics, was also communication *(śabdaḥ).* As we have seen, initially only brief explanations to the listed terms were given in these books. The same was the case with communication. The most common explanation for it was to define it as trustworthy instruction *(āptopadeśaḥ)* or as trustworthy tradition *(āptāgamaḥ).* This definition was retained even in later times, though the explanations gradually became more precise. Thus, e.g., Vṛṣagaṇa says in his *Ṣaṣṭitantram:* "He who is experienced in a subject and is free from error, is trustworthy with regard to it. His instruction is a trustworthy communication."[53] Here the explanation is expanded by a more precise definition of the term trustworthiness. Two things are emphasized in it. A reliable person is trustworthy when he has the necessary technical knowledge and when he is free from error - by error is to be understood, for example, indolence or malevolence. Thus, an advance forward was made. However, the development of the ideas prepared for here, first received importance and consequence in Nyāya.

Even the ancient textbook on dialectics, out of which the Nyāyasūtras later emerged, had mentioned communication under the instruments of valid knowledge and had said: "Communication is trustworthy instruction".[54] In his *Nyāyabhāṣyam* Pakṣilasvāmin explains it in the following way: "A teacher who knows the things clearly and who desires to communicate the object as he has seen it, is trustworthy".[55] Here, too, expert knowledge is mentioned as the first condition of trustworthiness, and the goodwill to communicate what was perceived in accordance with truth, as the second. Apart from this Pakṣilasvāmin remarks only that this is valid in the same way for the venerated

---

[53] *yo yatrābhiyuktaḥ karmaṇi cāduṣṭaḥ, sa tatrāptaḥ. tasyopadeśa āptavacanam.* [C/f. E. Frauwallner: "Die Erkenntnislehre des klassischen Sāṃkhya-Systems". WZKS 2, 1958, p. 124.]

[54] NSū I, 1, 7: *āptopadeśaḥ śabdaḥ.*

[55] NBh 26, 11f.: *āptaḥ khalu sākṣātkṛtadharmā yathādṛṣṭasyārthasya cikhyāpayiṣayā prayukta upadeṣṭā.*

teachers of the past, for the Aryans and the barbarians. He, therefore, hardly goes beyond what Vṛṣagaṇa had already said. But Nyāya did not stop with a mere explanation of the term communication. Soon other questions emerged which constantly led further on. Among these was the next question whether communication should at all be regarded as an independent instrument of valid knowledge.

Already since early times there were different opinions about the number of instruments of valid knowledge. Here also the phenomenon which we have already repeatedly come across reappeared, namely, that one attempted to understand a subject first by enumerating as completely as possible all its outward manifestations. Later on, however, one sorted them out, examined them and eliminated what did not belong here, so that the development led to greater simplicity, but also to greater clarity. Thus we find at the beginning a whole range of instruments of valid knowledge listed, from which many were removed, so that finally only a few were retained by the most important systems. Already in the Sūtras Nyāya taught only four instruments of valid knowledge: perception, inference, comparison, and communication. There were, moreover, also systems which acknowledged even fewer. Cārvāka, for example, regarded only perception as valid. This is due more to its fundamental standpoint, rather than to theoretical considerations. More important, however, was that Vaiśeṣika taught only perception and inference as instruments of knowledge, and that the Buddhists as well followed this view, as we have seen in Vasubandhu. This is the case because these schools were not satisfied with briefly rejecting the other instruments of knowledge, but rather based their view on earnest reasons. And, therefore, one had to discuss them.

We thus find already in the Nyāyasūtras, and with Pakṣilasvāmin, a discussion with opponents who stated that communication is not an independent instrument of valid knowledge.[56] They were rather of the opinion that this was merely a form of inference, and justified their view in the following way. Both inference and communication are concerned with knowing something unperceived through what is perceived. From the perceived smoke we infer the unperceived fire. We can experience unperceived things through the perceived word as well. Moreover, both cases are based on a relation *(sambandhaḥ)*, the knowledge of which makes it possible to know one through the other.

---

[56] NSū II, 1, 49-56.

The Nyāya answer depended above all on a distinction in the nature of the relation. It was said that the relation which is at the basis of an inference consists of a natural connection, of a contact *(prāptiḥ)* between the things in question. In fact, such a natural connection obtains between smoke and fire. In the case of a word and its object, on the other hand, such a relation does not exist, otherwise the object would have to be at the place of the word. Thus, by uttering the word fire, one would burn one's mouth. Or, the word and, together with it, the speech organs would be at the place of the object. But this is not the case. Therefore, in the case of a word and its object there is a different kind of relation, namely an agreement *(samayaḥ* or *saṃketaḥ),* which connects a specific word to a specific object. Such an agreement consists in "a stipulation of a fixed relation between naming and the named when one says: this object is named by this word".[57] If this stipulation is obtained, then one is able to know an object through a word, otherwise not. The science of grammar serves to preserve the agreement. That the relation between word and object is a matter of agreement, and not naturally determined, is further shown by the fact that it often happens that different people and nations use the same word for different things. Thus, the same word '*yavaḥ*' means barley for the Aryans and pepper for the barbarians. In this way, quite different conditions apply to communications and to inferences, and it is therefore unreasonable to regard them as the same.

These are some of the ideas we find in the Nyāyasūtras and in Pakṣilasvāmin. They, of course, led further. No sooner one began to consider more precisely the nature of communication and the state of the relation between a word and its object than other questions about linguistic matters arose on their own. Among these questions the most important ones were those concerning the nature of a word and of its object. We therefore already find both questions raised even in the Nyāyasūtras and by Pakṣilasvāmin, although their treatment is rather short and relies largely on old grammatical doctrines.[58]

The answer to the question about the nature of a word is, following Pāṇini, that sounds which terminate in an ending represent a

---

[57] Nbh 155, 19ff.: *kaḥ punar ayaṃ samayaḥ? asya śabdasyedam arthajātam abhidheyam ity abhidhānābhidheyaniyamaniyogaḥ.*

[58] This section of the Nyāyasūtras and the Nyāyabhāṣyam are dealt with in detail by Moritz Spitzer: "Begriffsuntersuchungen zum Nyāyabhāṣya, Leipzig, 1927 (Kiel dissertation).

word.[59] This definition covers both nouns and verbs. Prepositions and particles are regarded in it as nouns whose endings have been dropped. This is all that is said.

The treatment of the question about what is to be regarded as the object of a word is somewhat more detailed and more independent. As we have seen, ancient grammar was undecided as to whether the object of words was to be sought in individual things *(dravyāṇi)* or in its form *(ākṛtiḥ)*. We saw, further, that under the influence of the doctrine of categories which in the meantime had developed, there was a tendency to regard form as the same as class *(jātiḥ)*. In opposition to this, the Nyāyasūtras and Pakṣilasvāmin consider class as an object of words to be a third possibility, apart from individual thing and form. The question for them therefore was: are the individual things, their form, or the class inherent in them the object of words?

In their conception of these terms they come very close to Vaiśeṣika, although at this time Nyāya had not yet rejected its different natural philosophical standpoint.[60] Hence, for them an individual thing *(vyaktiḥ)* is to be understood as a substance *(dravyam)* which manifests itself to the senses as graspable and which is the locus of respective qualities - of specific qualities *(guṇaviśeṣāḥ)*, of general qualities and of limited extension. Form *(ākṛtiḥ)* is nothing but an arrangement *(vyūhaḥ)* of the parts of a thing and, furthermore, of the parts of these parts. The form also makes the class evident, although there are cases where this takes place independenty of the form. Class *(jātiḥ)*, finally, is what evokes the same idea with different things, through which, consequently, these very things are not different from one other. This, in fact, is merely generality *(sāmānyam)*, what in innumerable things is exclusively responsible for the agreement of knowledge. What, on the contrary, determines the non-difference of some things, as well as their difference from other things, is generality-particularity *(sāmānyaviśeṣaḥ)* or class.[61]

How is the question at hand now to be answered? Which of these three is the object of a word? In any case, something for and against may be advanced. When one speaks of a number of cows then this

---

[59] NSū II, 2, 57: *te vibhaktyantāḥ padam*. C/f. Pāṇini I, 4, 14.

[60] In the explanation that follows I am not distinguishing between the Sūtras and the Bhāṣyam, but I am generally following the advanced views of the latter.

[61] C/f. Vol. 2, p. 148 [English tr. Vol. 2, p. 104].

expression already shows that the word "cows" refers to several individual cows, and not the single class "cow". The same is true when one says: "He presents a cow", "The cow belongs to the Brahmin", etc. Here an individual thing would be the object of the words. On the other hand, the word cannot express the substance alone without the class which determines it more specifically, because there is no difference between the individual substances themselves. That the words are nonetheless used for the individual things may be explainable as some kind of transferred application. For the view that form is the object of words, it may be adduced that it [form] makes the difference among individual things possible, when one says: "This is a cow", "This is a horse". Nonetheless, it can be objected that words like "cow" also express class. Class does not, however, adhere to form but to substance. Finally, that class is the object of a word is indicated by the command "Bring a cow", which never refers to a clay figure, although class and form also obtain in it. But again, class by itself cannot possibly be an object of a word, because its appearance is determined by substance and form.

By way of a solution to these problems the Nyāyasūtras and Pakṣilasvāmin teach that all three, an individual thing, form and class, together constitute the object of a word, whereby the one, sometimes the other, is primary *(pradhānam)* or secondary *(aṅgam)*. If one wants to give expression to the particularity of a thing then the individual thing is primary, with form and class secondary. If one wants to give expression to generality then class is primary, with the individual thing and form being secondary. In this way, the relation is different from case to case.

This is essentially everything that the old Nyāya has to say about theory of language. We only need to discuss one more point which is most closely connected with communication as an instrument of valid knowledge, viz., the question about sacred tradition.

When communication was accorded an important place among the instruments of valid knowledge and dealt with in depth, it was not so much the usual communications in everyday life which were considered. These would have hardly aroused such an interest. It took place, rather, because sacred traditions or divine revelations were also understood as communication, to which so many schools appealed. Further, because the acknowledgement of their traditions was fundamentally important to these schools, the question of their trustworthiness was analysed in detail, and that is why the attacks of the opponents were as passionate as the defence.

From the very beginning Nyāya, no less than Vaiśeṣika, was not one of those schools which based its teaching on divine revelation. There is here, rather, an external element which subsequently had gained entry into the system. We saw in our presentation of Vaiśeṣika how Praśastapāda introduced the term God, although it was basically foreign to the system.[62] In exactly the same way the doctrine of a supreme God appears in Nyāya, without there being a compelling reason for it. It is similar to the acknowledgement of the sacred tradition, which was introduced although the system is not based on such a tradition and although not a single important teaching can be derived from it. The external element is quite obvious and we see here for the first time in the course of our exposition, signs of those powerful streams which gradually transformed the entire picture of Indian philosophy. This has to do with the important religious movements which largely replaced the old philosophical systems, or transformed them basically, and with the advance of brahmanical orthodoxy which, in association with these religious movements, led in time to the formation of Hinduism.[63]

In the case of Nyāya and Vaiśeṣika, moreover, we can trace where the religious influence originated from. There are, in fact, very early traces of a close relationship to the Śaiva sect of Pāśupatas. One of the ancient teachers of the school, whom we shall discuss below, is expressly referred to by the tradition as a Pāśupata master. A later teacher, Bhāsarvajña, also wrote a Pāśupata work, apart from his Nyāya writings. Further, in an old Sāṃkhya work, the *Yuktidīpikā*, the introduction of the term God in Vaiśeṣika is explicitly traced back to the influence of Pāśupata, even though in the ancient Vaiśeṣika system there is nowhere the mention of a supreme God.

If we inquire what the Nyāyasūtras and Pakṣilasvāmin say about sacred tradition, then it is not very much. Above all, the problem is not dealt with in its entirety. Only briefly is the trustworthiness of the Veda established and defended against attacks.[64] The justification for the trustworthiness occurs here in the following way. It is said: The trust-

---

62 Vol. 2, pp. 195f. [English tr. pp. 139f.].

63 C/f. Vol. 1, pp. 20ff. [English tr. pp. 11ff.].

64 For what follows c/f. NSū II, 1, 57-68.

worthiness of a tradition is recognized by its being verified in experience. In medicine, for example, trustworthiness is evident when, by the observance of the instructions, the indicated effect ensues. This, again, is due to the fact that the reliable people, on whom the tradition depends, are trustworthy. And their trustworthiness is, again, evident in that they have the necessary knowledge at their disposal, that they mean well with the listener, and that they wish to speak the truth. In this way, with these three qualities, the trustworthiness of reliable people is inferred, and from their trustworthiness, the trustworthiness of tradition is inferred. This is valid for matters of everyday life, as well as for the Veda. In the case of the Veda, on the other hand, the occurrence of the promised effect cannot, as a rule, be established through experience. Nevertheless, there are instances in which this is indeed possible, and from them it can be inferred that in all other cases the matter is not different. Moreover, the religious teachers who have preached the Veda, are the same as the preachers of medicine, the Āyurveda. It can be assumed that they are to be trusted in the one case just as in the other.

The main objections brought against the trustworthiness of the Veda are the following. It is maintained that the Veda teaches what is false. It can happen, for example, that one performs the son-ritual, for which the birth of a son is promised, without a son in fact being born. Further, the Veda contains contradictions. And, lastly, it has repetitions. Only those who do not clearly understand what they are saying repeat themselves. These objections were replied to thus: if the promises of the Veda are not kept then it is not because they are false, but because the instructions were not precisely followed. The apparent contradictions are due rather to a misunderstanding. And, as far as the supposed repetitions are concerned, they are not repetitions in a common sense but renewed repetitions *(anuvādaḥ)*, which serve a specific purpose and which are permissable.

Finally, a few words about the doctrine of a supreme God *(īśvaraḥ)*, since it can be traced back to the same influences as those of the recognition of the sacred tradition and since it later appears in close relation with this recognition. This doctrine is also not systematically expounded in the Nyāyasūtras, nor by Pakṣilasvāmin, but only appears occasionally in an excursus on language.[65]

[65] NSū IV, 1, 19-21.

In our presentation of the natural philosophical systems[66] we saw how the idea emerged to trace world events to the power of good and bad deeds *(karma)* of human beings, and how this idea received a very wide circulation. As opposed to this the view now began to appear that the deeds are not the ultimate cause, but a supreme God who controls everything. By way of justification it was said that the deeds of man do not always produce the desired fruit. From this it should be inferred that the occurrence of this fruit depends on some other cause, and this cause is God. This is not to mean that the deeds themselves are ineffective, but only that it is God who lets them come into effect.

To introduce the new view in this way is not very convincing. The justification is weak and Pakṣilasvāmin passes over it quickly. The strict law of the effects of deeds is thereby also violated. The old doctrine of the power of deeds and the belief in a supreme God could not be reconciled without contradictions. But the new religious streams were quite powerful and asserted themselves despite all objections and reservations.

Accordingly, the nature and function of God were thought of in the following way. By nature God is a soul *(ātmā)*, because, as with all the other souls, he is inferred on the basis of the qualities of knowledge *(buddhiḥ)*, etc.[67] The divine soul is, however, distinguished from the other souls by possessing merit *(dharmaḥ)*, knowledge *(jñānam)* and concentration *(samādhiḥ)* in the highest degrees, whereas non-merit *(adharmaḥ)* erroneous knowledge *(mithyājñānam)* and inattention *(pramādaḥ)* are alien to it. As a result of merit and concentration it possesses, furthermore, eight abilities *(aiśvaryāṇi)* or miraculous powers: to make itself arbitrarily small or big, light or heavy; to cover distances; to fulfill its desires; to control nature; and to choose places and forms of life at will.[68] God operates in that he instigates the elements and in that he lets the merit and demerit which attach themselves to the individual souls to come into effect. In this way he is the supreme cause, without the deeds of man thereby becoming ineffective.

Suffice it to say this much here, because this subject will still be often discussed, especially with the presentation of the religious systems. We have, at the same time, fully dealt with what the old Nyāya

---

66 Vol. 2, pp. 91ff. [English tr. Vol. 2, pp. 61ff.].

67 C/f. Vol. 2, pp. 210f. [English tr. pp. 150f.].

68 C/f. Vol. 1, p. 373 [English tr. p. 295].

had to say about the question concerning communication as an instrument of valid knowledge and about language theory. This is not very much, nor is the content very significant. What is important, however, is that through this a complex of problems was taken up by the system, because another crucial development was to follow from it.

We shall now turn to a system which has dealt with language-theoretical questions in the greatest detail and in a most unique way, viz., Mīmāṃsā. The starting point for Mīmāṃsā was, above all, the question about the validity of the sacred tradition, the Veda. However, before we turn to this question we need to go further back because, even though the philosophical elements in Mīmāṃsā are later, it is still necessary to have a glance at the early development. Only in this way will it be understandable why philosophical ideas entered the system at all and why they took on such remarkable ways.

As we have observed at the beginning of our presentation of the philosophy of the Veda,[69] the Vedic sacrifice was extremely complicated. This was due to the fact that the sacrifice came to be seen very early as a magic deed which brought about a desired effect with magic power. This was so because, through this, every detail became especially important since it was magically powerful and influenced the result. Thus, intricate sacrifices were developed which often lasted a long time and employed a large number of priests. It was also quite natural under these circumstances that a literature soon emerged for the purpose of describing and explaining the sacrifice. As we have already said, three kinds of priests were active in the Vedic sacrifice: the Adhvaryuḥ who performed the sacrificial rite, the Hotā who recited the sacred hymns to it, and the Udgātā who sang the songs of the sacrifice. Each of these kinds of priests possessed a collection of sacred texts: the Adhvaryuḥ the collection of the sayings, the Yajurveda, with which he accompanied the sacrifice; the Hotā the ancient collection of hymns of the Ṛgveda; and the Udgātā the collection of melodies of the Sāmaveda. These three collections, the three Vedas, were carefully transmitted in school-like institutions. In these very schools of priests there emerged descriptions of the sacrifices and explanations about their secret meaning, in the socalled Brāhmaṇas. Step by step these grew into elaborate works. Thus, in the course of time, there developed an extensive science of sacrifice.

---

[69] Vol. 1, pp. 39ff. [English tr. pp. 27ff.].

Gradually, however, problems began to arise. The Brāhmaṇas themselves, which in the meantime also came to be regarded as sacred texts, proved to be inadequate for the study of sacrifices, because from the very beginning they served more as an explanation of the secret meaning of the sacrifice, rather than as a description of its performance. Besides, they were continuations of the individual Vedas and therefore dealt with the sacrifice only from the point of view of the one respective group of priests. Moreover, each of the Vedas was transmitted in numerous schools and each school had its own Brāhmaṇa which often noticeably differed from those of the other schools.

These problems led at first to the emergence of a separate Vedic auxilliary science, the science of rituals *(kalpaḥ)*. It attempted to provide a systematic description of each sacrifice, and this was done in different textbooks in the form of mnemonics, of sūtras, which in the meantime had become conventional. In this way innumerable ritual sūtras originated in the Vedic schools, which gave a significantly clearer and more systematic description of a sacrifice than the ancient Brāhmaṇas. However, all difficulties were not yet removed by this alone. The ritual sūtras, further, presented the sacrifice from the standpoint of a particular group of priests only, and these too were different according to the different schools. And, above all, it was not possible to ignore the ancient texts of the Brāhmaṇas which in the meantime gained recognition as divine revelation. One had to derive everything finally from these incomplete and often contradictory sacred texts. And thus a new science grew which taught how the desired knowledge could be obtained from the sacred writings, viz., the science of interpretation of Mīmāṃsā.

The Mīmāṃsā school also has a long history. It took a long time from the earliest discussions about ritual questions as we find them already in the Brāhmaṇas, to the development of sound principles of interpretation, until a clear idea of the nature of sacrifice was gained, until the interpretation of the sacred writings was reconciled with it, and until all the detailed questions which arose at each stage were thoroughly discussed and clarified. All this presupposes a long, school-like activity. The knowledge which was thereby obtained was reflected, as was customary at that time, in a comprehensive collection of mnemonics, the Mīmāṃsāsūtras of Jaimini.[70] The time of this collection cannot at present be exactly determined. As with other similar collections it emerged gradually and was continuously changed and elaborated. The only really definite point in the development we can grasp here is from the oldest extant commentary to the Sūtras, Śabarasvāmin's Mīmāṃsābhāṣyam, which belongs to about the fifth century. Beyond this only a predecessor of Śabarasvāmin, whom he calls Vṛttikāra (the writer of a Vṛttiḥ, a short commentary) is known and from whose commentary he reproduces quite a large section, especially in the discussion on epistemology. The following sketch of what was philosophically significant in the old Mīmāṃsā is on the basis of Śabarasvāmin and his reports concerning the views of the Vṛttikāra.

As we have seen, the aim of Mīmāṃsā was to obtain definite information about religious duty from the sacred tradition, above all about the sacrifices prescribed in the Veda. However, before proceeding with an interpretation of the sacred tradition there were a few preliminary questions to clarify. It was important to determine above all what in fact was decisive, as a sacred tradition, for the knowledge of religious duty.[71] There could be no doubt as regards the revelation *(śrutiḥ)* which were contained in the collections of sayings and hymns and in the Brāhmaṇas. Apart from these, however, there was also a huge mass of other transmissions *(smṛtiḥ)*, be they in the form of respected works or time-honoured custom. How should one consider them? The following was decided. This tradition by itself was not given any authority. Authority can only be concluded when there is reason for the assumption that the tradition in question is traceable to Vedic texts, and this applies even to a text that may no longer be extant, or when the benefit of the traditional prescriptions is obvious. In no case, however, is a tradition valid if it contradicts revelation, or if it can be traced back to ignoble motives, such as brahmanical avarice. It is noteworthy that the ritual sūtras were not themselves regarded as revelation: because they were transmitted imperfectly without the accent signs of Vedic texts, because they do not present the material in the form of prescriptions, but in a descriptive form, and also because they repeatedly contain contradictions of the texts of revelation.

---

[70] C/f. the sketch of the Mīmāṃsā literature, Vol. 2, pp. 23-25 [English tr. pp. 9-11].

[71] MBh on sūtra I, 3.

Another preliminary question concerned the Vedic revelation itself. This was composed of components of the most various kinds. It was therefore necessary to obtain clarity about how to evaluate the individual parts. Initially the entire Veda was divided, as already stated, into collections of sacred hymns and sayings which were summarized under the name of formulas *(mantrāḥ)* and into the descriptive writings of the Brāhmaṇas. Of these, the formulas say nothing about religious duties because they do not describe the sacrifices, but are themselves a component of the sacrifices or of other religious deeds. It is significant that there could be the view that the formulas, as regards their content, are completely meaningless.[72] It would only be important that they be mentioned at all. Finally, however, the view prevailed that the formulas are meaningful. And since it was not desired that any part of the Veda be regarded as being without significance for the knowledge of religious duties, it was said that the value of the formulas was that they name the components of the sacrifice and draw attention to them. Nevertheless, the significance of the formulas for Mīmāṃsā is minimal. What is interesting are only a few rules of interpretation which were developed in connection with the concern with the formulas.[73]

As for the formulas in prose, viz., the sayings of the Yajurveda, the separation of the individual sayings was not always easy, and there could often be quite different opinions regarding them. Therefore, in order to come to a clear decision in such cases it was necessary to construct sound rules about what is to be regarded as a unitary sentence and what not. This was handled in the following way. It was said: "A sentence is a unit if it serves a single purpose and, in the case of a separation, requires (completion)".[74] Thus, the essential part of a unitary sentence was that it expresses a complete thought, and that in the case of an analysis the parts are incomplete and cannot stand independently. On the other hand, it was permitted to analyse a row of words into several sentences if it is made up of many independent elements. In this case the possibility of completion was also taken into consideration. It was said that if a group of words refers to several equally important elements of a sentence, then it is permitted to connect it with each of these elements and, thereby, to derive several independent sentences.

---

72 MBh on sūtras I, 2, 31-53.

73 MBh on sūtras II, 1, 46-49.

74 MSū II, 1, 46: *arthaikatvād ekaṃ vākyam, sākāṅkṣaṃ ced vibhāge syāt.*

However, this is not allowed if the equally important elements are separated from one another by other words not belonging to them. These clear and completely rational principles could be applied usefully not only by Mīmāṃsā.

Now, to consider the Vedic texts most important for Mīmāṃsā, the Brāhmaṇas: these too contain various kinds of components. What Mīmāṃsā sought in them was a clarification of religious duties, especially those about the Vedic sacrifices, viz., which ones were to be performed and in what way. The precepts *(vidhiḥ* or *codanā)* contained in the Brāhmaṇas supplied these clarifications. But the precepts did not at all make up the entire content of these works. The largely greater part is of a completely different kind and does not have anything to do with precepts directly. Thus, here too one was confronted with the question how these parts of the Brāhmaṇas were to be understood and what significance they have, because it was impossible to regard a large portion of the divine revelation as meaningless.

The following was the procedure to solve these questions.[75] The parts of the Brāhmaṇas which did not contain any precepts mainly offer factual explanations *(arthavādaḥ)*, i.e., explanations of and reasons for the precepts, or other further considerations as well. Taken literally they therefore contain no statements about religious duties and are, consequently, useless from the Mīmāṃsā point of view. But this could not possibly be accepted. Under these circumstances the only way out was in fact to put them in some relation to the precepts, to explain them to a certain extent as supplements to the precepts *(vidhiśeṣaḥ)*. And this indeed was done. It was said that the technical explanations contain a eulogy of the sacrifice or of what is associated with it. In this way they allow the performance of the sacrifice to appear desirable and, thus, they support the precepts. If the wording did not favour such an interpretation then one adopted a metaphorical or figurative expression and did not even hesitate here to give forced interpretations. In this way practically everything which was not itself a precept could be explained. Only a few individual words and expressions in the precepts remained, which were regarded as names *(nāmadheyam)*. Their purpose was seen as what defined the sacrifice more precisely and, thereby, as what brought about the relation to a particular fruit of a sacrifice and to

---

[75] MBh on sūtras I, 2, 1-30.

particular aids.[76]

The preliminary questions have thus been dealt with and we can now proceed to the actual core of Mīmāṃsā, the Vedic precepts *(vidhayaḥ)*. Its art of interpretation unfolds completely here. The most important precepts were those which prescribed the preformance of a sacrifice. There were often cases in which it was doubtful whether the precept in question prescribed a separate sacrifice with its own fruit, or whether it was merely related to a sacrifice previously mentioned. Six guiding principles were taught here, from which it could be inferred that a separate sacrifice is prescribed[77]: the use of different words in the precepts in question *(śabdāntaram)*, repetition of the same words *(abhyāsaḥ)*, the mention of a number *(saṃkhyā)*, difference in the aids *(guṇaḥ)* to be used in the different sacrifices, the context in which a precept appears *(prakaraṇam)*, and the use of different names *(nāmadheyam)*. In other cases it was a question of the relation of the members of the sacrifice *(aṅgāni)*, i.e., the subordinate acts and aids, to the main performance. Again, six means *(pramāṇāni)* were taught in order to know this relation in the transmitted texts.[78] What is decisive in the first place is a direct declaration of revelation *(śrutiḥ)*. Other guiding principles are word meaning *(liṅgam)* and sentence relation *(vākyam)*. In other cases, again, the questionable relation is to be deciphered from the context in which the precepts in question appear *(prakaraṇam)*, from their sequence *(kramaḥ)*, or from the nomenclature used in them *(samākhyā)*. The rule that applies here is that the preceeding means is always more conclusive than the later ones. Other rules again teach how the sequence of the different sacrificial performances is to be known from the texts.[79] Here too a direct declaration of revelation *(śrutiḥ)* is above all decisive. As a second resort sense and purpose *(arthaḥ)* of the different performances decide the case. Other guiding principles are derived from the sequence of the reference in the sacred texts *(pāṭhaḥ)*, and several other similar ones.

Suffice it with this brevity to have already given an idea of how Mīmāṃsā proceeded with its exegesis of Vedic texts. Of course, one was not, thereby, satisfied with constructing such general rules. Their

---

[76] MBh on sūtra I, 4.
[77] MBh on sūtras II, 2-3.
[78] MBh on sūtras III, 2-3.
[79] MBh on sūtras V, 1.

application in discussing and deciding numerous individual cases occupies the main part of the Sūtras and the Bhāṣyam. Thus, a significant achievement was accomplished methodologically. It was learnt how to interpret difficult texts according to strict rules. And this achievement could become fruitful for other areas as well. This in fact did happen. Indian law, especially, learnt a great deal from Mīmāṃsā about the interpretation of the ancient law books. All this has nothing to do with philosophy. And that is why Mīmāṃsā would not deserve a place in the history of Indian philosophy. Only the following ideas came close to philosophical questions.

The Mīmāṃsā method of interpretation described above made it indeed possible to determine the construction of the sacrifices on the basis of the Vedic texts. But this was not everything that was required. What was inferred in this way was an established, but arbitrary, construction. However, the Vedic sacrifice, as we have often said, was a magical performance which was to compel a certain result. But this was conceivable only as a very specific, concerted effect of its parts. The efficacy of the sacrifice, therefore, presupposed a necessary, intrinsic connection of its parts. This intrinsic connection, the organic structure of the sacrifice, had to be ascertained if one were to be sure about the proper performance and, thereby, of the success.

In order to be clear about this it was necessary at the outset to answer the following question[80]: How can a sacrificial performance which, in fact, is only a procedure that is over quickly, produce an effect which appears only at a much later time - since it is impossible for an effect to become manifest when its cause has long since ceased to be present? No completely new problem, however, was raised with this question. In fact, we already came across a similar question, namely, with the doctrine of the consequences of good and bad deeds *(karma)*.[81] There too it was necessary to explain how a deed performed long previously bears fruit only later in a new rebirth. Among the several attempts at an answer we became acquainted with there, was also the one by Vaiśeṣika. It assumed that deeds produce an imperceptible power, called the invisible *(adṛṣṭam)* which, on its part, produces the effect at the appropriate time. The way in which Mīmāṃsā proposed a solution to its problem was very similar to this. It too supposed that

---

[80] MBh on sūtra II, 1,5.

[81] C/f. Vol. 2, p. 92 [English tr. p. 61].

the sacrificial performance produces an invisible power which later ripens the fruit of the sacrifice. But it chose another name for it, calling this power the previously non-existent *(apūrvam)*.

With the supposition of what is previously non-existent only one problem was at first solved. New questions immediately emerged. The Vedic sacrifice is indeed very much a combined procedure and requires various kinds of aids. How, one has thus to ask, do these produce the previously non-existent? Or, does each produce separately its own previously non-existent?

In order to arrive at a clear decision here different parts of the sacrifice were first distinguished. These are, apart from the various sacrificial deeds and the people who perform them, the numerous objects *(dravyāṇi)*, offerings and utensils. Very often the qualities *(guṇāḥ)* of these objects also play a role. Finally, especially with the offerings, a preparation *(saṃskāraḥ)* was also often necessary. It was decided that of these the objects and qualities do not separately produce what was previously non-existent, because they fulfil their purpose in that they serve the sacrificial performance. According to a generally accepted rule, however, one should not presuppose any invisible effect as long as a visible one can be proved. But, also, not all deeds produce what was previously non-existent.[82] This is valid especially for deeds which are for the sake of the preparation of the sacrificial objects, because their purpose is fulfilled with this preparation. Only those deeds which do not have such an object as their aim, produce what was previously non-existent. Anyhow, there are numerous such deeds within the sacrifice itself. That is why a great number of previously non-existents arises which, finally, together produce a single previously non-existent, which in turn brings forth the final fruit of the entire sacrifice.

In this way the structure of the sacrifice began to be outlined in its main features. The sacrifice presents itself as a series of main performances which, through what was previously non-existent, produce the fruit of the sacrifice, and to which everything else was organically attached as ancillaries *(aṅgāni)* or as supplements *(śeṣaḥ)*.[83] But how was this structure to be read from the words of the Vedic precepts?[84]

---

82 MBh on sūtras II, 1, 6-8.

83 C/f. MBh on sūtras III, 1, 1-6.

84 For what follows c/f. MBh on sūtras II, 1, 1-4.

In order to achieve this it was asked at the outset whether in the Vedic precepts - which prescribe the attainment of a specific fruit with the help of a sacrifice through the production of what was previously non-existent - the production of what was previously non-existent is prescribed by every word or only by a single word. The answer given was: only by a single word. If indeed the production of what was previously non-existent is prescribed just by one word then everything else which the other words express can be related to this single one and brought into connection with it. Therefore, in this case, only the assumption of a single previously non-existent is necessary. And a generally accepted rule states that among various possible assumptions those are always to be preferred which presuppose the least unknown factors.

But which is the one word which prescribes the production of what was previously non-existent? One of the nouns and adjectives *(dravya-* and *guṇaśabdāḥ)* which appear in the precept, or the verb? The answer was: the verb, or as it was stated, the word of action which expresses becoming *(bhāvārthaḥ karmaśabdaḥ)*. The following was the justification for this. Words of action require completion *(ākāṅkṣā)*, because when something is to be done one asks what, by what means and how. The answer is provided by the other words of the sentence which are thereby combined with the word of action and satisfy the need for completion. Such a need, however, obtains only with words of action, and not with nouns and adjectives. As nouns *(nāmāni)* substantives and adjectives are in fact words by the use of which one perceives an object. They therefore have as an object *(bhūtārthaḥ)* something that has already come to be and, thus, something existing. The words of action, i.e., the verbs *(ākhyātāni)*, on the other hand, are words which are not applied to any existing object. They thus have something that is yet to be as their object *(bhavyārthaḥ)*. Now, what has already come to be can indeed fulfil its purpose in the service of what is yet to be, in that this can be produced through what has already become, but not vice versa. And that is why nouns and adjectives, which express what has already come to be, have no need for completion. Thus, it is a verb or word of action which in the Vedic precepts prescribes the production of what is yet to be, since only with it can the remaining words of the precept be connected in order to satisfy the need for completion, so that the assumption of a single previously non-existent is sufficient.

In trying now to analyse and to interpret a Vedic precept in accordance with the developed views the result was the following. Let us take for example the simple precept: "Whoever desires heaven should sacrifice" *(yajeta svargakāmaḥ)*. Here, the verb, i.e., the word of action which expresses something yet to be *(bhāvārthaḥ karmaśabdaḥ)* prescribes, at the outset in general, the occasion of what is yet to be *(bhāvanā)* and thereby requires several supplementations. Above all, whose yet-to-be is to be occasioned or, stated briefly, what should be produced? The answer is to be read in the precept itself. It is heaven, which the sacrificer desires. And since heaven cannot be produced directly the production of a corresponding previously non-exixtent is to be regarded as the first aim. The next supplement concerns the question through what means. This is supplied by the word of action itself, because to sacrifice means to occasion what is to be through a sacrifice. Finally, with the saying "whoever desires heaven" *(svargakāmaḥ)* the above precept points to the bearer *(āśrayaḥ)* of the deed, the sacrificer. Correctly understood the precept therefore means: through the means of the sacrifice the sacrificer should produce a previously non-existent and through this, heaven.

In this way the core of the above-mentioned structure of the sacrifice is given: the production of a previously non-existent and, moreover, of the desired fruit by the sacrificer through the means of the sacrifice. Everything else for a further interpretation of the precept could easily be associated with this core as an auxilliary or a supplement. In this way an interpretation of the precepts was arrived at, which corresponded to the acquired views concerning the structure of a sacrifice.

With these ideas, moreover, linguistic questions were also touched upon. It became necessary to distinguish different kinds of words and to explain their differences. In the case of a verb a distinction was made between the general verbal character and what was expressed by the verbal stem. Then one began to consider how the single words in a sentence are connected to and supplement each other. These were the beginnings of the concern with linguistic questions. This was not very much, especially in comparison to the concurrent development in the schools of grammarians. But the beginnings were in themselves important because of the later development which continued from them.

We have thus discussed all the necessary points concerning the Mīmāṃsā doctrine of interpretation of the exegesis of Vedic texts and we come now to the questions which lead to pure philosophy, to questions of epistemology.

Originally, in fact, epistemology, as with philosophy itself, was completely alien to Mīmāṃsā. The Veda as sacred revelation was given for it, firmly believing in its validity, and all efforts, therefore, turned around an understanding of it. It was only the attacks of the opponents which compelled it to justify its own belief in the Veda, and this led step by step deeper and deeper into epistemological questions until, finally, these were investigated and dealt with in detail and penetratingly, as with any other philosophical system.

In order to understand this discussion properly we have to bear in mind what the Veda was for Mīmāṃsā. And we can understand this better, in turn, if we begin with its views on sacrifice. As we have often repeated, the sacrifice was for it a magical deed which necessarily compels the result. It was thus believed that forces were active in the sacrifice which, like the forces of nature, operate according to inexorable laws. And these laws were found stated in the Veda. This means, however, that for Mīmāṃsā the Veda was neither the revelation of a divine will nor, much less, the work of any human being. Rather, it was seen as a self-given expression of eternal natural laws. That is both, the Veda and the natural law, were seen as eternal and intransient.

It is quite understandable that this interpretation soon became the object of attacks from all circles which did not believe in the Veda. Later it was so with the religious sects too which, while not denying the trustworthiness of the Veda, explained it, however, as the creation and revelation of God. It was therefore necessary to defend oneself against these attacks. Two points were central here in this debate: the thesis that the Veda is not the work of any human being *(pauruṣeyaḥ),* but rather uncreated and eternal and, secondly, the question about its trustworthiness.

As far as the eternality of the Veda is concerned, the objections of the opponents were based above all on isolated observations which seemed to speak for the view that the Veda is of human composition and indeed of a relatively later time.[85] Thus, it was pointed out that the text collections of the Vedic schools have been transmitted under specific names which represent derivations of names of persons. It was said that this is to be traced back to the fact that these persons were the composers of the collections in question. Thus, for example, in one place it is stated *babara prāvāhaṇi*. This means "the son of Pravāhaṇa cheri-

[85] MBh on sūtras I, 1, 27-32.

shed the desire". It was rightly pointed out, however, that such texts could have been composed only after the lifetime of the person in question and could therefore not be eternal.

The first of these objections was relatively easy to reply to. It was said that the persons whose names the Vedic collections bear, did not compose these collections, but that they played a special role in their transmission and that is why their names were associated with them. It was more difficult to reject the second objection. But here, too, one was not nonplussed, in that it was said that these cases were not names of people. Prāvāhaṇi, for example, does not refer to the son of Pravāhaṇa but means, according to its etymology, "one who carries forth", and this is a reference to wind. The word *babara* too is merely an onomatopoeic name for wind. Therefore, there is no reference to a human person but to the eternal wind, which does not contradict the eternality of the Veda. Furthermore, one was not satisfied with refuting the hostile objections but, rather, one attempted to justify one's own position independently. That the Veda is not a human work, it was said, is derived from the fact that no composer for it has been transmitted. And this is also not a case of it being merely forgotten; because the Vedic sacrifices require so much time and are so costly that in order to justify its performance one would have definitely always appealed to the authority of the composer, if there were one and if the Veda were not an eternal, uncreated natural law.[86]

Much more difficult than this justification of the eternality of the Veda was the debate on the second problem about the question of its trustworthiness. Here, the course of the discussion led to ever new questions, and deep into the area of language theory and, finally, to epistemology in general.

The reason why a decisive significance was given to this problem was that the Vedic precepts were regarded as the only means for the knowledge of religious duties because, it was said, perception is limited to the present.[87] However, by fulfilling religious duties, especially by performing the Vedic sacrifice, it was a matter of achieving aims denied to every kind of perception, and about which only the Veda can provide information. This was so because the doctrine of Sāṃkhya that, through inference, one can know things beyond the domain of every

[86] C/f. for example, Jayanta, NM [I 214, 25ff.].

[87] MSū I, 1, 4.

kind of perception was, at the time these discussions took place, not yet propounded.

But how is it now possible to justify the trustworthiness of the Veda? At the outset this did not seem to offer much difficulty. The guarantee for its trustworthiness was already seen in the fact that it was not a human composition, but uncreated and eternal, because it was believed that in this way all errors, which are due to human deficiency, are excluded. Thus, every occasion to doubt the correctness of its assertions is eliminated. Soon, however, doubts arose. Even if the words of the Veda are eternal and transmitted by human beings since beginningless time from generation to generation, the meaning of the words are conditioned by the sense one gives them. According to general opinion this is done by people. This is continuously evident in everyday life in cases of giving names, in which a particular name as a designation for a particular person or thing is stipulated. In this way the statements of the Veda must indeed depend on people finally.

In order to dispel these doubts one of the oldest Mīmāṃsā and Vedānta teachers, Bādarāyaṇa, had already propounded the following theory: The relation between word and object does not depend on human consensus, but is naturally given *(autpattikaḥ)*, i.e., the origin of a word is simultaneous with the relation to its object. Man's role is limited to communicating this relation.

In order to understand the significance of this theory we have to bear in mind that we are here concerned with a time, which we have also come across when dealing with the doctrines of the grammarians, in which, with regard to judgements on linguistic matters, there was then no awareness of the intellectual processes which were involved but, rather, were considered only external, real things. Thus, the words which communicate an object could be placed on the same level as the sense organs which enable the perception of its objects, or as a lamp which illuminates things. If one now takes into consideration that the words of the Veda were regarded as existing independently as such, then with the theory that the relation to objects is naturally given, namely, that the words by their very nature are able to express objects, every human intervention is in fact eliminated. Thus, the trustworthiness of the Veda could be seen as established.

In order to reinforce Bādarāyaṇa's theory several justifications were put forward. So it was said[88]: the relation between a word and its object is eternal because we do not know its author. Even if he belongs to the distant past one would surely remember him, because only in the case of insignificant works is a creator forgotten. It may happen with a house, a garden or a well that the land in question is devastated, that the family which owns them becomes extinct and that, thereby, who built and designed them is forgotten. Language, on the other hand, has never been distinct from man, so that tradition cannot be disconnected. The necessity to remember the creator of the relation between a word and its object is evident, furthermore, in the technical expressions of grammar and prosody which one understands only if one knows the different head-masters and their terminological system.

From the fact that one does not understand words on hearing them for the first time, but has to be first taught which objects they refer to, it cannot be conclusively inferred that the relation between a word and its object was created by human beings, because there is also the possibility that one is merely taught the natural relation already existing between them. And just as children learn this relation from the speech and deeds of older ones, so too did they themselves learn this relation in their youth from their elders, and so on since beginningless time. It is to be borne in mind, further, that an artificially created relation would not be adopted everywhere, up to the remotest regions. Finally, the establishing of such a relation presupposes the use of words for which a relation already exists. The same is also valid in their case, and so forth always, without ever coming to an end.

In this way it was believed that the doctrine of the naturally given relation between a word and its object was adequately justified and, thereby, the validity of the Veda established. But very soon another doubt arose.[89] Everything that has been said till now is valid only for the relation between a single word and its object. In the case of Vedic precepts, however, it is not a matter of individual words but sentences. And what a sentence expresses, is quite different from the mere objects of individual words. This is evident already in the fact that the object of a word is something general, the object of a sentence is something particular. For example, the word cow by itself refers to cow in general. The sentence: "Devadatta, bring the white cow", on the other hand,

---

[88] MBh I, 10, 5-9; 11, 31-13, 25.

[89] C/f. MSū I, 1, 24-26.

refers to a single, particular cow. The particular object of the sentence here is not expressed by one of the words which make up the sentence, nor through a new word inserted in it, but rather through the totality of the words which constitute it. However, there does not exist an eternal relation between this totality and the object of the sentence. Besides, the word constructions of Vedic sentences do not occur in everyday life, so that the relation with its object cannot be learnt from everyday use of language. In both sentences and their objects, therefore, it is a matter of artificial constructions. That is why there is human influence and the possibility of error.

In order to refute this objection it was pointed out that the objects of different words of a sentence mutually determine and influence each other. The object of Vedic precepts is, above all, a deed which is expressed by a verb. The other words of the sentence are connected with this verb, and this determines the object. Thus the ideas, as they were applied, became ways so as to derive the structure of the sacrifices from the linguistic form of the Vedic precepts.[90] However, it follows from this that the object of the sentence automatically emerged from the objects of the individual words. This means, further, that between the individual words and the object of the sentence no human involvement intervenes. Sentences may be formed in the language of everyday life by people, in the case of the eternal precepts of the Veda [on the other hand] the individual words make it possible, through the eternal relation, to recognize their object, and the various objects constitute the object of the sentence and, moreover, without human intervention. In this way the trustworthiness of the precepts as sentences is also established.

Everything said thus far, from the eternality of the relation between a word and its object to the doctrine that the objects of words form the object of the sentence automatically, constitutes an intellectually coherent, self-contained unit. With this, the efforts to prove the trustworthiness of the Veda reached their first conclusion. Soon, however, other ideas were associated with them. With the assertion that the relation between a word and its object is eternal, the area of language theory was entered into. It now went step by step, deeper into it. One question asked very early was about the object of words. We have already seen how this qestion was dealt with in grammar. Mīmāṃsā

---

[90] C/f. pp. 104ff. above.

worked with the same ideas but viewed things from a different standpoint. As with everything else, here too the main point for Mīmāṃsā was the interpretation of the Vedic precepts. And in this case, as well, it judged the things accordingly.

Mīmāṃsā also began with the question whether a word expresses a concrete, individual thing *(dravyam)* or the form *(ākṛtiḥ)* common to all things of the same kind. Form was decided upon, since it was said: if, with regard to an artistic arrangement of the fire altar, it is stated "one is to lay a falcon arrangement" then the arrangement of real falcons is not meant, but the arrangement in the form of a falcon. Soon, however, the terms were changed. In the place of form, even if the old names were retained, 'universal', which is intrinsic to things, was used, similar to the term generality *(sāmānyam)* of Vaiśeṣika. And for individual things, instead of the old expression which had taken on the meaning 'substance' a new term was chosen which expresses the individual appearance *(vyaktiḥ)*. The problem thus took the following form: does a word express the universal or the particular? For Mīmāṃsā, however, for whom everything was a matter of interpreting the Vedic precepts, this meant: do the Vedic precepts give intructions of a general character, or are they concerned only with individual things?

Initially, the views on this were diverse.[91] To some extent, it was decided that words express individual things. In this case attention was especially drawn to the fact that the deeds prescribed in the Vedic precepts are directed at individual things. If, for example, it is stated, "an ox is to be offered, a he-goat for Agni and Soma", then the sacrifice is to be performed on individual animals. There were also some arguments against the theory that form, i.e., the universal, is the object of words. It was said that the one form cannot indeed at the same time attach itself to different bearers, just as a person cannot at the same be in different places. If, further, a word expresses form then it would mean that all dogs died when one talks about the death of one dog. We see that individual things are different, even if one uses a single word for them, and that is why we also speak of them separately. Finally, it is evident in the case of homonyms, where the same word refers to different things, that the object of the word cannot be of the same kind.

Ultimately, the opinion that form is the object of a word did pre-

---

[91] For what follows compare Patañjali's *Mahābhāṣyam* on I, 2, 64, vt. 35-39 who in my view here draws from a Mīmāṃsā source. C/f. WZKS [4, 1960, 92ff.].

vail over this view. It was justified on the grounds that the same word evokes the same idea, that the different individual things which it expresses cannot be distinguished by the word; and that a word once used for a particular object can later easily refer to objects of the same kind. It was finally maintained that the rules in law books too do not refer to individual cases, but have general validity. It was also believed that the objections of the opponents could be refuted without difficulty. For the view that the same form is inherent in different bearers the example of the sun was referred to, which is seen by different people in different places at the same time, or that of the god Indra who is called to several sacrifices at the same time and is present at all. That not all dogs die with the death of one dog is based on the fact that the form, i.e., what is common to all dogs, does not firmly attach itself to individual animals and that is why it does not perish with them. The difference among objects expressed by the same word and the fact that one speaks of objects separately, is due to the difference in individual things. Finally, with homonyms, that different things are referred to by the same word can be traced back to the fact that there is indeed something of the same kind behind this designation.

Despite all this, however, the objection was not refuted that the Vedic precepts direct the performance towards individual things, thus the precepts have to express them in some way.[92] Consequently, it was always attempted to vindicate the theory of individual things as objects of words. It was sought in the following way to meet the objection that words do not in fact refer only to such an individual thing, but that they are also used for others. It was said that the individual things, like substance *(dravyam)*, are mere bearers of different generalities *(sāmānyāni)* and particularities *(viśeṣāḥ)*, without itself being further determined. Therefore, a word could refer to numerous individual things irrespective of the particularities inherent in it. But this assertion was easy to refute because it was difficult to justify why under these circumstances a word does not refer to any arbitrary, individual thing, but only to those which fall within the area of a particular class.

The following assertion was to be taken more seriously: words refer to individual things insofar as they are determined by some form. However, the knowledge of a particular naturally presupposes the knowledge of the particularizing factor. And that is why words express

---

[92] For what follows c/f. MBh on I, 3, 30-35.

both the individual thing and the form. Nonetheless, they express the individual thing chiefly *(prādhānyena)* and form, on the other hand, only secondarily *(guṇabhāvena)*.

However, even with regard to this attempt at a solution, the theory already propounded that only form is the object of a word, was finally retained. It was said that an individual thing and form are not expressed simultaneously by the word, but that an individual is known only because it is always connected with form. A word, therefore, enables one to know only the form, and only thereafter the individual thing, because of the constant connection.

The concern in all these discussions, as already stated, was a question which occupied Mīmāṃsā from the early times. However, although this question directly concerned the theory of language, it had in fact relatively little significance for development of it within Mīmāṃsā itself. This was quite different with another doctrine which belongs to a somewhat later stage of the development of the system, and which represents one of the most unique and controversial theories of Mīmāṃsā, namely, the doctrine of the eternality of sound.[93]

---

[93] For what follows c/f. MSū I, 1, 6-23. Also, WZKS [5, 1961, 113-124].

## 4. Mīmāṃsā
## [BA/VI/1-4]

However justified the method of Mīmāṃsā has been and however important it became for large areas, all this has nothing to do with philosophy. The Mīmāṃsaka was convinced that the implementation of the Vedic injunctions leads to salvation and he asked how it was to be performed. At first there were no other considerations. The impetus for a preoccupation with philosophical questions came from outside, through the objections of those who did not believe in the Veda. In confronting them it was necessary to prove the truth of Vedic revelation. This led to a consideration of epistemological questions and further, step by step, to a discussion of other philosophical problems till, finally, to an attempt to formulate them within the framework of a proper system.

Whoever had broken away from the belief in the sanctity of the Veda and had begun looking at its teachings with a critical eye must have soon found several things questionable in it. Thus, various objections ensued. Among others, these were directed more particularly against the promises which were linked to the accomplishment of the Vedic sacrifices. Thus, for example, one Vedic precept said that whoever desires cattle should perform the Citrā sacrifice. And so it was said[94]: What lies in the field of perception but is not in fact perceived, does not exist, like the horn of a hare.[95] The sense organs, however, would be in a position to perceive cattle. However, after performing the Citrā sacrifice they do not perceive any cattle. Therefore, this sacrifice does not bring cattle as a result, since the result of a deed has to be evident at the same time as the deed itself, just as the pleasant sensation aroused by a massage appears during the massage. One could, however, suppose that the sarifice would produce its result afterwards. But this is not the case because at the time of the sacrifice it did not yield its result. If the result will be produced [later] then the sacrifice is no longer present. How can the sacrifice, then, produce its result when it is already over?

Further, several statements of the Veda contradict experience. For example, among the precepts for the burial of a sacrificer it is stated: "The sacrificer, equipped with the sacrificial paraphernalia, goes directly

---

94 According to MBh. I, 8, 23ff. I am deliberately following the form of the Sanskrit text to a large extent here.

95 This is a favourite example for something completely unreal, since a hare does not have a horn.

to the world of heaven". This evidently refers to the corpse to which the paraphernalia are attached. However, it does not go to heaven, but is incinerated in front of those present. Such a statement, then, contradicts experience, in the same way if one were to say: "Gourds sink in water, whereas stones float". If such statements prove to be false then one will also not trust those which promise heaven as a result of a sacrifice.

The Mīmāṃsakas sought to justify the credibility of the Veda against such attacks and they tried to do it in the following way. They said: the statements of the Veda are correct because the sources of mistakes, which are responsible for error in human communication, are absent in the eternal Veda. And the Veda is eternal because the word is eternal.

These ideas, which were basic for later Mīmāṃsā epistemology, are already expressed in the oldest extant commentary to Jaimini's Sūtras, the *Mīmāṃsābhāṣyam* of Śabarasvāmin, and also by an earlier commentator from whose work Śabarasvāmin quotes a long section in his commentary, by the socalled Vṛttikāra.[96] Much of this is insufficient and questionable, especially with Śabarasvāmin, who was indeed a good ritualist but not a philosophical thinker. However, we find here in broad outline the direction indicated, which the later thought of the school pursued. We therefore have to deal more in detail with the views of Śabarasvāmin and the Vṛttikāra.

Their starting point is the following question: Dharma, viz., the religious duties whose fulfilment leads to well-being in this and in the other world, is known from the Vedic precepts. But who tells us that these precepts are reliable and that the Veda does not also state what is incorrect, as with human communication?

This is the answer[97]: The statement "it states what is incorrect" entails a contradiction. "It states" means, "it enables one to know; it is the cause that one knows something", because the presence of that by which, as a cause, one knows something, this enables knowing. Therefore, if with the existence of a Vedic precept one knows: "the heavenly reward ensues from the sacrificial fire", how can one say that this is not so? Or, if it is not so, how can one know? - because, to say that one knows something non-existent, is a contradiction.

96 C/f. the details on Mīmāṃsā literature in Vol. 2, pp. 23f. [English tr. pp. 9f.].

97 Here too, I am closely following Śabarasvāmin's wording for the decisive sections.

## 5. [The Vṛttikāra's Theory of Language] [BA/VII/43-45]

The presentation of the instruments of knowledge and, at the same time, of the entire epistemology is concluded with [the discussion of] the non-existent. It constitutes a complete, self-contained unit. Nevertheless, much of it is short and sketchy. The doctrine of communication, especially, is treated rather briefly. This is due to the fact that the Vṛttikāra wanted to devote a detailed presentation of the Mīmāṃsā theory of language separately. And this follows immediately after the epistemology.

He effects the transition in such a way that he lets an opponent raise the objection that the other instruments of knowledge may indeed be valid but that communication and, thereby, the Veda as an instrument of knowledge, does not come under consideration because the Vedic promises as regards the fruit of the sacrifices are not true and, besides, that some statements of the Veda are in direct contradiction to experience. He refutes this objection with a proof of the trustworthiness of the Veda. He does this by furnishing a proof in a traditional manner, by which he shows that the statements of the Vedic precepts are free from any human influences and, consequently, that there can be no doubt as regards its trustworthiness. And this gives him the occasion also to discuss in detail the Mīmāṃsā theory of language, as far as it was developed till then.

First he deals with a discussion of the question why the exclusion of human intervention guarantees the trustworthiness of the Veda. His answer is the following. If communication depends on people then one can doubt its correctness. If, on the other hand, as it is in the case of the Veda, the word speaks for itself, then it conveys the knowledge of its object directly, like a sense organ. One oneself, therefore, directly arrives at a knowledge of the object in question. Thus, this knowledge is equal to that obtained by sense perception. A sense perception, however, as it was taught at that time[98], is an instrument of valid knowledge, if it is neither doubtful nor erroneous. The knowledge which an unequivocal Vedic precept gives rise to, is not doubtful. Nor is it erroneous, because it cannot be contradicted by any other knowledge of the same kind at another time, at another place, under different situations or by any other person. Further, one cannot infer the error of Vedic statements from the error of other communications, because an inference

---

98 C/f. the definition of Nyāya above [in the incompleted part which was to follow the first sketch]; *avyapadeśyaḥ* of the Vṛttikāra is not clear.

does not prevail over against the direct certainty which perception provides. And the knowledge which the statements of the Veda convey, as said, is to be regarded as perception. Therefore, the Vedic precepts have to be regarded as being just as valid as instruments of knowledge as a sense perception.

Then follows a discussion of linguistic questions which is intended to justify the eternality of the Vedic words and the eternality of the relation with their objects.

What at the outset concerns the nature of words, the Vṛttikāra follows Upavarṣa's theory mentioned above, according to which a word is nothing else but the sounds of which it consists. Objections were raised against this theory on the side of the schools of grammar, as we came across it with the justification of the theory of suddenness *(sphoṭaḥ)*. It was said that it is impossible that a word can produce the knowledge of its object in this way, because the sounds individually are not capable of it. Nor do they constitute a unit because each sound already disappears with the production of the following sound. The Vṛttikāra refuted this objection by saying that despite the transitoriness of the sounds and despite the fact that they do not constitute a unit, a co-operation is possible. Each sound leaves behind a memory impression *(saṃskāraḥ)*, and these sounds, together with the last one, produce the knowledge of an object. In reply to the opponents he says, further, that the sounds are indeed perceivable, but not the unitary word presupposed by them. Their theory therefore goes against the basic principle that one should not take recourse to invisible factors when explaining an appearance, as long as what is visible is sufficient for an explanation.

With regard to the objects of words as well, the Vṛttikāra followed the traditional views, even if he supplemented them on individual points.

## 6. Kumārila
[BA/VIII/2, 5-6]

We shall now turn to the problems which make up the core of Mīmāṃsā philosophical thinking and see what form they have taken with Kumārila. At the very outset we have to ask about the trustworthiness of knowledge in general because, as our presentation of the old Mīmāṃsā has shown, this had already become the basic question for the Vṛttikāra, on which the proof for the trustworthiness of the Veda depends. Kumārila's treatment of the question is characterized by the following trends. He follows the ideas of the old Mīmāṃsā. However, what were still uncertain, tentative attempts there, have been developed by him into clear, precisely formulated principles, which he defends with the entire acumen of his dialectic, through which in fact the weakness of his position also becomes quite clear.

As for the question about the nature of a word, Kumārila essentially does not go beyond Śabara. For him, too, a word is nothing else but the sounds of which it consists; what concerns him is only a substantiation and justification of this theory. He thereby carries the ideas further and outlines another entire series of various possibilities.[99]

The main point is, again, the question about how it is possible that sounds, without really forming a unit, can produce the single effect of the knowledge of an object. Kumārila says here: even though sounds may be incapable of producing their effects individually, this does not mean that they are not able to do this together. We see clearly with parts of a wagon that they are not suitable for transporting a load individually, whereas together they are easily in a position to do so. In the case at hand, the sounds make up a unit insofar as certain sounds together are capable of producing the knowledge of a specific object. This unit, further, is characterized by the following features. The sounds in it are closely joined *(sāhityam)*, they follow each other in a definite sequence *(kramaviśeṣaḥ)*, and they are produced by a single speaker *(ekakartṛtā)*. The theory regarding this, viz., that the sounds following each other in sequence are in a position to produce a single effect was, as we have already seen,[100] rather vehemently attacked on the part of the opponent, because by uttering a sound the previous ones are already past and are therefore incapable of operating. In answer to this Kumārila says: just as there are causes which operate simultaneously, so too there are those which operate consecutively. In this way the

---

[99] *Ślokavārttikam* 15, vv. 65-136.

[100] C/f. p. 121 above.

deeds following each other in sequence in a sacrifice produce the single effect of the fruit of the sacrifice. And with studies, only repetition evinces the desired result. In such cases the real cause is the last cause. This does not say anything against the efficacy of the previous ones, even if they are separated from the effect by links in between.

Thus, despite the hostile objections Kumārila reckons with the possibility that the sounds following each other in sequence produce the single effect of a knowledge of the object. He also allows for the possibility, which Śabara had already assumed, that the previous sounds produce impressions in the knowledge *(saṃskārāḥ)* and that these together with the last sound are the cause of the single knowledge, so that, as the opponent demands, the simultaneous cooperation of all sounds is given. He explains this in the following way: it is generally accepted that every vivid perception leaves behind an impression in the knowledge, which later may produce a memory. In our context here, the impressions would not in fact have memory as a consequence but, rather, the knowledge of the object of the word in question. There is, however, no objection to this because the causal connection is thereby established, that the knowledge ensues on account of these impressions. If, as the opponent demands, one now wants the sounds following each other in sequence simultaneously to produce the knowledge of the object, then there is the possibility that the previous sounds which continue to exist in the form of impressions, produce this together with the last sound. There is also the possibility that all the sounds are first grasped in a particular knowledge which on its part is the cause of the knowledge of the object. This knowledge can either grasp the last sound directly and the previous ones with the help of the impressions left behind, or for all sounds, including the last one, this can be based on the impression. This is similar to counting where the knowledge of the last number is based on the knowledge of the earlier smaller numbers and the impressions left behind thereby. Whatever the case may be in detail, the demand of the opponent is satisfied.

## 7. Dharmakīrti
]BA/IV/27-35]

Dharmakīrti's concern begins with a logical problem, and one taken over from Dignāga. Dignāga's most important achievement in the field of formal logic was the clear handling of the relation between reason and consequence by pointedly demarcating their areas. He first achieved this in his *Hetucakraḍamaruḥ* and then in his later works elaborated it in all its consequences. In this way, as we have seen, the basis for a correct inference was created. But there was especially one weakness in his theory. With a demarcation of the area of reason and consequence only their external relation was determined, an inner connection was not thereby given. Further, the determination of the external relation was based only on experience, whose fragmentariness one had to reckon with. And despite Dignāga's efforts to dispel these doubts, one question was repeatedly raised: is it sufficient to determine the relation between reason and conclusion by observing a series of cases experientially, and does such a determination guarantee the unconditional correctness of an inference? What was achieved as regards inferences after Dignāga's time, especially on the part of the followers of Nyāya, may have raised doubts. Only too often it happened that those inferences which adhered to the conditions set up by Dignāga led, however, to consequences which appeared to be unacceptable from the Buddhist standpoint. And indeed it was not easy to prove from experience the incorrectness of the assumed relation between reason and consequence.

This is where Dharmakīrti begins. He starts with the insight that the determination of the external relation between reason and consequence on the basis of experience is inadequate in order to vindicate the correctness of an inference, but that there must be an internal connection between both. This knowledge was not completely new. We find indications of it already before Dignāga. Especially Vṛṣagaṇa had already assumed an inner connection between reason and consequence and he had taught that there are seven kinds of relations which make an inference possible. But initially Dignāga did not pay attention to it because of the satisfaction with his own insights. And later he turned to other ideas which led him to the theory of imaginative knowledge and of a term. Further, Vṛṣagaṇa's theory had weaknesses, which had to make its rejection appear justified. Most of the relations enumerated by him do not present reliable connections. The things so related can appear together, but this does not necessarily have to be the case.

Thereby, the reliability of an inference based on it is in question and has, at most, probability value.

As opposed to this Dharmakīrti demands that an inference be based on necessary relations which do not permit any exception *(vyabhicāraḥ)*, and he attempts to determine what relations satisfy this demand.

He believed that he found such a relation especially in the causal relation which joins two things together as cause and effect. He taught that it is possible, thereby, to infer with certainty the existence of a cause from the existence of the effect, because there cannot be an effect without a cause. The inference from a cause to an effect is, however, uncertain because even if the cause exists, unforeseen hindrances can well make the emergence of the effect impossible. We find similar ideas already expressed in the old logic. Early Nyāya had already explained an apriori inference *(pūrvavad anumānam)* as an inference from a cause to an effect, and aposteriori inference *(śeṣavad anumānam)* as an inference from the effect to the cause,[101] and Vṛṣagaṇa had expressly stated that the aposteriori inference, i.e., the inference from the effect to the cause, is valid *(avyabhicāri)* without exception.[102] But Dharmakīrti goes further.

He first poses the question about how it can be ascertained that two things stand in a relation to each other as cause and effect. He answers this in the following way: if something that was not perceived previously, although the conditions for its perception were given, is perceived because of a perception of another thing, but is not existent if this other thing is absent even if all other conditions are given, then it is the effect of this other thing.[103] This is to be understood in this way: we do not first perceive an effect, although in fact it would be perceivable; then a cause emerges and accordingly the effect appears as well. The effect, on the other hand, is absent when the cause is absent, even if all other conditions for its emergence are fulfilled.

One could object to this by saying that under these conditions the determination of the causal relation is itself based only on an observation of experience, just as with Dignāga's determination of the concurrent appearance of cause and effect, and that here too experience has to

---

[101] NBh 23, 8-11; see above [not supplied].

[102] "Die Erkenntnislehre des klassischen Sāṃkhya-Systems", WZKS 2, 1958, p. 128; see above [not supplied].

[103] C/f. HB 4*, 8-12; PVSV 22, 2f.

be fragmentary and the consequence based on it therefore uncertain. But Dharmakīrti's answer to this is: this is not the case because if we have determined the concurrent appearance of two things in several cases, then it does not mean thereby that they in any case also must appear together. If, on the other hand, we have determined as certain the causal connection between two things only once, then this is valid without exception for all other cases, because what is recognized as an effect can never emerge without its cause.

But is the causal relation really valid without exception in all cases? Dharmakīrti also deals with this question. And here we see for the first time, and what is to become evident repeatedly, how he goes to the base of things and attempts to carry his ideas through to their final consequences. He says: the things of the world of appearance are caused, otherwise they have to be eternal or never existent at all, because whatever does not require an external influence for its existence exists always and forever. Or, if it does not exist then it cannot be produced. Thus, all things of the world of appearance are connected with a cause which determines their being and their nature. This means that their essence is determined by the fact that they are produced by a certain cause and that the things in turn produce a certain effect. Consequently, the causal connection is firmly rooted in the essence of things and this is valid unconditionally and without exception.

In order to understand this properly we have to remember the following as well. The Buddhist schools of the classical time, and especially also the Sautrāntika school on whose views Dharmakīrti relies in the first place, do not accept any permanent things, neither matter *(prakṛtiḥ)* as in Sāṃkhya, nor substances *(dravyāṇi)* as in Vaiśeṣika but, rather, only fleeting appearances which arise and perish in a moment. What is the nature of these appearances? Vaiśeṣika terminology cannot be applied here because the distinction between substance *(dravyam)* and qualities *(guṇāḥ)*, and especially the case of generalities *(sāmānyāni)*, are mere ideas for the Sautrāntika doctrine. The above mentioned appearances, however, are not ideas, but real. What is then their nature and, above all, what distinguishes them from the ideas as real?

Here the term efficaciousness now has a meaning. What is real is effective. There was a similar idea in another context. In the school of the Sarvāstivādins, which taught that not only the present things but also the past and future ones are really existent, what distinguished the present things from the past and future ones, was seen in their effectness *(kāritram)*.[104] In the same way Dharmakīrti now believed that the essence of the real things which distinguishes them from ideas is to be found in their effectness, that they are in a position to produce a desired effect *(arthakriyākāritvam)*. Every fleeting appearance out of which the world of appearance is constituted, according to his view, is thus by nature a certain effectness. It is in a certain sense an energy moment which in the very next moment causes a specific effect.

With this we understand why, according to Dharmakīrti's view, the causal effect is rooted in the very nature of things, and we also understand the definitions he gives of cause and effect. A cause, he says, is what according to its nature produces a certain effect *(tathābhūtakāryajananasvabhāvaḥ)*, and an effect is what according to its nature is produced by this cause *(tajjanyasvabhāvaḥ)*. Thus, fire is what produces smoke; smoke is what is produced by fire. Here, it is not a matter of what names of linguistic use one applies to the various things. What the effectness in question entails is fire, whatever else one may call it, because it is the effectness which constitutes the nature of a thing.[105] Where, however, different causes appear to produce the same effect, it can in fact be seen at a closer examination that in reality several effects are involved. Thus, a flower which grows out of a bulb is created differently from the one grown from a seed.[106] Finally, it is to be noted, also, that there is never a single cause which produces a certain effect but, rather, always a totality of causes *(sāmagrī)*. And it is therefore this totality which is inferred from the effect, because it is in its nature to produce this effect.[107]

So, Dharmakīrti arrives at the following formulations:[108] "cause and effect are characterized by the fact that, by their nature in relation to each other, they are the producer and the produced. If, therefore, even smoke were to be created by something else, other than the totality of causes, fire, etc., then by its very nature it would not be produced thereby and, consequently, would not be produced even once, just as with any other thing. And this totality of causes would not produce it,

---

104 C/f. Vol. 3 (Saṃghabhadra) [c/f. preliminary remarks, p. 63 above].

105 PVSV 23, 10ff.

106 C/f. PVSV 23, 22-25; PVin II 36*, 22-27.

107 PVSV 23, 19-21.

108 HB 20*, 4-16 [translated from the Tibetan].

because it would not be in its nature to produce it, as with any other totality of causes. ... Thus, what produces smoke is the specific totality of causes, fire, etc., and what is produced by the particular totality of causes fire, etc., is smoke. Since, therefore, cause and effect are in this way closely connected to each other by nature, the production from something else is not possible. Consequently, there cannot be an effect without its cause."

This is the first fixed relation between cause and effect which Dharmakīrti determined. It is based on the causal relation between two things and makes possible the inference to a cause from an effect. Dharmakīrti calls it the reason through effect *(kāryahetuḥ)*. He believed he found a second kind of fixed relation in the following case.

In his attempt to clarify the relation in the areas of reason and conclusion, Dignāga came to the conclusion from the cases he particularly investigated that it was a matter of ideas *(kalpanāḥ)* in narrower or broader areas, where the area of the one encompasses that of the other, and he derived these ideas and their various scopes from the various exclusions of the other *(anyāpohaḥ)*.[109] Now it is clear that in such a case the encompassed idea enables a definite inference of what is encompassing. But how is it that both ideas are connected to each other in such a way? As in all cases, Dignāga derived its relation through observation in experience. This did not satisfy Dharmakīrti. In these cases one cannot talk of a causal relation. It was therefore necessary to prove another kind of fixed relation, if such an inference is to be valid.

Here, Dharmakīrti now believed he found the reason for the fixed relation in the fact that the one and the same thing is at the basis of both the ideas which represent reason and conclusion. Let us take as an example the inference that often serves as a model: "This is a tree, because it is an elm".[110] The object of the inference here is a specific tree, i.e., a single, real thing. Tree and elm, on the other hand, according to the theory of exclusion of the other, are ideas which are derived from this for the demarcation from certain other things. In this way the one real thing is, to a certain extent, divided into various properties *(dharmāḥ)*, of which two serve as reason and consequence in our case. In reality *(vastutaḥ)* they have only one single thing as their base, and it is this unity of being *(tādātmyam)* which necessarily joins them to each

---

[109] C/f. above [not supplied].

[110] Indians give as example the Śiṃśapā tree *(Dalbergia Sissoo)*.

other.

Thus, the relations in the case of such an inference are the following. The consequence belongs to the intrinsic nature *(svabhāvaḥ)* of the reason. It belongs to the nature of an elm that it is a tree. With the existence of a thing, however, what belongs to its nature is also necessarily given. If there is an elm, then there must be a tree. Dharmakīrti calls this a reason from intrinsic nature *(svabhāvahetuḥ)* and formulates it thus: "The intrinsic nature serves as the reason when the quality to be proved is given with the mere existence of the proving quality."[111]

But here too Dharmakīrti was not completely satisfied with this knowledge alone, but asked further: are these qualites which serve as reason and consequence really connected to each other through a unity by nature, and is it possible to furnish a proof for this? According to the Buddhist theory of exclusion of the other, the position is clear. But for a follower of Nyāya the things appeared quite differently. For him the individual things constituted a collection of different entities which belong to different categories. Therefore, reason and consequence were also different entities for him. In the case of the inference above, this does not make much of a difference, because one could hardly deny the relation between elm and tree. It was, however, different for example in the case of the inference which was especially important for Dharmakīrti, viz., to infer their transience *(anityatā)* from the being-caused *(kṛtakatvam)* of things. Here one could ask oneself if the being-caused of things necessarily in fact entails their transience, as it is maintained on the part of the Buddhists. Nyāya, in any case, represented the view that transience is produced only afterwards, after the origin of things, through external causes. So it was necessary here to prove the assumed unity of essence, if being-caused and transience are to serve as reason and consequence.

For this purpose Dharmakīrti again went back to the theory of causality. As we have seen, the essence of a thing for him rests in its efficaciousness and is in turn determined by the fact that it is produced by certain causes. The nature of a thing is thereby determined by its causes. Different causes produce different effects because, as he said, "the difference or the cause of the difference among things is due to the fact that they possess contradictory qualities or have different

---

[111] HB 5*, 10f.: *sādhanadharmabhāvamātrānvayini sādhyadharme svabhāvo hetuḥ.*

causes".[112] On the contrary, the same causes produce the same things. And what originates from the one and same totality of causes *(sāmagrī)*, is one and the same thing. The same totality of causes which produces the things as caused, also produces them as transient.[113] Being-caused and transience are, therefore, inseparably united in one and the same essence and only in our imagination do they appear as two different factors, by reason of exclusion of the other. Consequently, they can serve as reason and consequence in an inference, and through this unity of their essence, such an inference is compelling.

---

[112] PVSV 20, 21f.
[113] PVSV 17, 21ff.

## Abbreviations and Bibliography


| | |
|---|---|
| AS | *Abhidharmasamuccayaḥ* (Asaṅga), ed. Prahlad Pradhan (Visva-Bharati St. 12). Santiniketan, 1950. |
| Vol. 1 | *Geschichte der indischen Philosophie I.* Salzburg, 1953. [English tr. by V. M. Bedekar: *History of Indian Philosophy*, Volume I, Delhi, 1973, repr. 1984]. |
| Vol. 2 | *Geschichte der indischen Philosophie II.* Salzburg, 1956. [English tr. by V. M. Bedekar: *History of Indian Philosophy*, Volume II, Delhi, 1973, repr. 1984]. |
| CS | *Carakasaṃhitā*, ed. Yādava Śarman. Bonbay,1933. |
| HB | *Hetubinduḥ* (Dharmakīrti), ed. E.Steinkellner. Wien, 1967. |
| MBh | *Mīmāṃsābhāṣyam* (Śabarasvāmin), ed. Ratna Gopal Bhatta. (KSS 42) Benares 1910. |
| MSū | *Mīmāṃsāsūtram.* |
| NBh | *Nyāyabhāṣyam* (Pakṣilasvāmin), ed. Lakṣmaṇa Śāstri, Śrīrāma Śāstri. (KSS 43) Benares, 1920. |
| NM | *Nyāyamañjarī* (Jayantabhaṭṭa), ed. S. N. Śukla. (KSS 106) Benares, 1936. |
| NSū | *Nyāyasūtram.* |
| P | *The Tibetan Tripitaka.* Peking Edition, ed. D.T. Suzuki. Tokyo-Kyoto 1955-1961 (reprint). |
| PVin II | *Pramāṇaviniścayaḥ* (Dharmakīrti), Ch. 2, ed. E. Steinkellner. Wien, 1973. |
| PVSV | *Pramāṇavārttikasvavṛttiḥ* (Dharmakīrti), ed. R. Gnoli. (Ser. Or. Roma 23). Roma, 1960. |
| VSū | *Vaiśeṣikasūtram.* |
| WZKS | *Wiener Zeitschrift für die Kunde Süd (Vol. 1-13: und Ost)asiens.* |
| YD | *Yuktidīpikā*, ed. P. Chakravarti. (CSS 23). Calcutta, 1938. |

## Appendix A
## [R/II/1]

... therefore the affectionate treatment of him.

Such a blending of the separate history of a school with the history of the original community, and the link of its headmaster with the old patriarchs is not an exception, rather the rule. Often as a pre-history, especially with the missions, are: a visit to the country by the Buddha and a prophecy made by him; early councils and lines of patriarchs linking up with starting points; legends of the leading headmaster. (History of conversion or founding of the synod.)

1. The Upagupta Legend (similarity noticed by Przyluski: *La légende de l'empereur Açoka dans les textes indiens et chinois*, Paris, 1923, 111f:

2. The Madhyāntika Legend.

The same here with hardly any variation: instead of the missing prophecy made by the Buddha, here there is one by the Arhat of the second council; for the general part, report on the first and second councils (interpolation?); list of patriarchs (after the first council, as with Upagupta); then, as a separate part Apadāna Moggaliputta's: 1. Moggaliputta's youth, 2. the third council, 3. the missions; terminated, because here the Ceylonese church history is inserted.

## Appendix B
## [R/III/11]

### Composition of the Ancient Mahāvaṃsaḥ

**1. Prehistory** (Buddha's visit to Ceylon): D 1-2[1]
**2. Rājavaṃsaḥ** (Prehistory to the Chronicle?): D 3
**3. The Church History**
- **A: in the Motherland:**
  1. The First Council: D 4, 1-26; 5, 1-14
     Ācariyaparamparā: 4, 27-46; 5, 69-107
  2. The Second Council: D 4, 47-53; 5,15-29
     Formation of the Sects: 5, 30-54
  3. The Third Council: D 7, 34-43 and 44-59
     The Prehistory: 5, 55-68
     The Story about Asoka: 6, 1-7, 23
  4. The Missions: D 8
- **B: in Ceylon:**
  1. Tissa and Asoka: D 11, 15-12, 7
  2. Mahinda's Arrival: D 12, 7-13, 25
  3. Founding of Tissārāma: D 13, 26-14, 40
  4. Rainy Period and Founding of Cetiyārāma: D 14, 55-80
  5. Establishing the First Stūpa: D 15, 1-73
     (the four Buddhas in Ceylon: 15, 34-73)[2]
  6. Planting the Bodhitree: 15, 74-17, 74
     (the four Buddhas in Ceylon: 17, 1-74)[3]
  7. Founding of the local Ācariyaparamparā:
     D 16,38-40 (c/f. Smp!); 18, 1-44
     (Mahinda's Death: 17, 95-109)

**4. The Chronicle:**
1. The Earliest Period: D 9,1-11, 5
2. Since Muṭasīva: D 11, 6f. + 17, 75f. + 79-94; 18, 45 - End

**Chronological Concordances:** D 3, 51-61: c/f. Ācariyaparamparā; 6, 19-21 (etc.?); 7, 24-33; 11, 8-14; 17, 77ff.

---

[1] This presupposes the chronology of the *Nidānakathā*.

[2] The story about Mahinda is incorporated in the basic store of the motherland.

[3] Probably belongs originally to 5. and was later moved to 6 (Bodhitree), because the old Stūpa retreated into the background, whereas the Bodhitree had still retained its meaning for the monks of Mahāvihāra.

## Appendix C
## [BA/XI/18-20, 12]

### The Philosophy of the Indians
### Part 1

Foreword.

§ 1 The Classification of Indian Philosophy.

§ 2 The Tradition.

**I. The Philosophy of the Earlier Period.**

**A. The Early Period.**

§ 3 The Philosophy of the Vedah.

§ 4 Period of Transition. The Philosophy of the Epic. Yogaḥ.

§ 5 The Buddha and the Jina (Ājīvikāḥ).

**B. The Period of the Systems.**

§ 6 Sāṃkhyam (Yogaḥ).

§ 7 Vaiśeṣikam.

§ 8 Lokāyatam.

§ 9 The Formation of the Systems in Buddhism. Abhidharmaḥ.

§ 10 Sautrāntikāḥ.

§ 11 The Madhyamaka Doctrine.

§ 12 The Idealism of Yogācārāḥ. § 12 b The System of the Jainas (Umāsvātiḥ).

**C. The Aftermath.**

§ 13 The Vāda Handbooks. Nyāyaḥ.

§ 14 Mīmāṃsā.

§ 15 The Logical School of the Buddhists. (Logic of the Jainas).

## The Philosophy of the Indians
Part 2

### II. The Philosophy of the Later Period.

**A. The Continuation of the Ideas of the Vedaḥ and the Beginnings of Vedāntaḥ.**

§ 1 The Earlier Upaniṣads (Bhagavadgītā).

§ 2 The Language Philosophy of the Grammarians.

§ 3 The Beginnings of Vedāntaḥ. Śaṅkaraḥ and Maṇḍanamiśraḥ.

**B. The Religious Sects and the Systems of the Śaivas.**

§ 4 Pañcarātram (Purāṇam).

§ 5 Pāśupatam (and other Sects of the Śaivas).

§ 6 The Śaiva System.

§ 7 The Pratyabhijñā System.

§ 8 The Southern Śaivasiddhāntaḥ

§ 9 Liṅgāyatāḥ.

**C. The Conclusion of Buddhism and the Tantric Schools.**

§ 10 The Conclusion of Buddhism. Buddhist Tantrism

§ 11 The School of the Nātāḥ. (The Kaula Doctrine).

§ 12 The Śāktas.

**D. The School of Śaṅkara and the Vedānta System of the Vaiṣṇavas.**

§ 13 The Later Saṅkara Vedāntaḥ.

§ 14 The Viśiṣṭādvaita Doctrine of Rāmānujaḥ. (Modified Monism).

§ 15 The Dualism of Ānandatīrthaḥ.

## Appendix D
## [BA/XII/1]

### Plan of Volume 4

**I. The Beginnings.**

1. **Dialectics:** The Vāda Handbooks. Nyāyaḥ. Synthesis with Natural Philosophy, the Sūtras, Pakṣilasvāmī.
2. **Academic Systematization:** Tantrayuktayaḥ, Epistemology of Sāṃkhyam, Vṛṣagaṇaḥ (Vindhyavāsī).
3. **Language Philosophy:** Grammar, Bhartṛhariḥ, Mīmāṃsā, Development of Language Philosophy; Vṛttikāraḥ – Śabaraḥ.

**II. The Completion.**

1. **The Buddhist Attempts,** Vasubandhuḥ, **Dignāgaḥ.**
2. **Vaiśeṣikam;** Beginnings, Praśastapādaḥ.
3. **Nyāyaḥ:** Basic Transformation Through the Adoption of Vaiśeṣika Natural Philosophy, Ācāryaḥ – Vyākhyātā, Uddyotakaraḥ.
4. **Mīmāṃsā:** Kumārilaḥ and Prabhākaraḥ.
5. **Dharmakīrtiḥ** (Īśvarasenaḥ).

**III. The Aftermath.**

1. **Dharmakīrti's School:** Dharmottarah;, Prajñākaraguptaḥ, Jñānaśrīmitraḥ (Ratnakīrtiḥ).
2. **Nyāyaḥ:** Śaṅkarasvāmī, Trilocanah, (Jayantaḥ), Udayanaḥ and his School.
3. **Mīmāṃsā:** Maṇḍanamiśraḥ, Umbekaḥ, Sucaritaḥ, – Śālikanāthaḥ.

**To be Included:** Cārvāka Epistemology.

# INDEX